MADE BY HAND

FURNITURE PROJECTS FROM THE UNPLUGGED WOODSHOP

TOM FIDGEN

POPULAR WOODWORKING BOOKS
CINCINNATI, OHIO
www.popularwoodworking.com

MADE BY HAND. Copyright © 2009 by Tom Fidgen. Printed and bound in China. All rights reserved. No part of this book may be reproduced in any form or by any electronic or mechanical means including information storage and retrieval systems without permission in writing from the publisher, except by a reviewer, who may quote brief passages in a review. Published by Popular Woodworking Books, an imprint of F+W Media, Inc., 4700 East Galbraith Road, Cincinnati, Ohio, 45236. 800-289-0963. First edition.

Distributed in Canada by Fraser Direct
100 Armstrong Avenue
Georgetown, Ontario L7G 5S4
Canada

Distributed in the U.K. and Europe by David & Charles
Brunel House
Newton Abbot
Devon TQ12 4PU
England
Tel: (+44) 1626 323200
Fax: (+44) 1626 323319
E-mail: postmaster@davidandcharles.co.uk

Distributed in Australia by Capricorn Link
P.O. Box 704
Windsor, NSW 2756
Australia

Visit our Web site at www.popularwoodworking.com.

Other fine Popular Woodworking Books are available from your local bookstore or direct from the publisher.

13   12   11   10   09   5   4   3   2   1

Library of Congress Cataloging-in-Publication Data

Fidgen, Tom.
  Made by hand : furniture projects from the un-plugged woodshop / Tom Fidgen. -- 1st ed.
    p. cm.
  Includes bibliographical references and index.
  ISBN 978-1-55870-895-2 (hardcover : alk. paper)
  1. Furniture making--Amateurs' manuals. 2. Woodworking tools--Amateurs' manuals. I. Title.
  TT195.F53 2009
  684'.08--dc22

2009023421

Acquisitions Editor: David Baker-Thiel
    (david.thiel@fwmedia.com)
Senior Editor: Jim Stack
    (jim.stack@fwmedia.com)
Designer: Brian Roeth
Production Coordinator: Mark Griffin
Photographer: Tom Fidgen

ABOUT THE AUTHOR

Tom Fidgen builds custom furniture using hand tools and fine hand selected hardwoods. He is a contributing author to *Woodworking Magazine* and has written for *Fine Woodworking* and *Popular Woodworking*.

METRIC CONVERSION CHART

to convert	to	multiply by
Inches	Centimeters	2.54
Centimeters	Inches	0.4
Feet	Centimeters	30.5
Centimeters	Feet	0.03
Yards	Meters	0.9
Meters	Yards	1.1

ACKNOWLEDGEMENTS

First off I'd like to express my deepest thanks to everyone at *Popular Woodworking* for making this project a reality; especially Megan Fitzpatrick who contacted me way back when and started this crazy ball-a-rollin'. And to David Thiel my editor, who allowed me such freedom right out of the starting gates. Cheers to you!

To my beautiful wife Carolyn and our amazing children, Nelson and Piper for being my pillars of strength through these lonely eight months; yes Nelson, "Now Daddy has some time to play!" As you grow older and look back on these pages, I want you to know how much those early morning workshops visits meant to me. You'd always say, "Daddy that cabinet is looking GREAT!" It was those little words of encouragement that kept me on track. In a few years when you get a little older we'll be making shavings together!

Thanks are also needed for the inspiration that was sparked in me at such a very young age when I would sit and watch those Saturday afternoon television broadcasts back home on Cape Breton Island. Roy Underhill, Norm Abram and Bob Ross; thinking back, it's funny how these television personalities can creep into a young mind. Seriously though, who didn't dream of that woodshop in the trees, across the brook and away from the rat race? From there came the tools, all of those power tools — and in front stands a humble but likeable gentleman in flannel. And through it all, I can still recall Bob Ross. You know the painter guy with the 'killer 'fro', a kind of John Denver cool, reminding and instilling a slower pace at which to work. "A little tree here and a little brook there..." tread lightly.

To the hallways of education in public spaces where I quite literally stumbled over a book in a Halifax Library; *A Cabinetmakers Notebook* hmmm ... James Krenov eh? Never heard of him but it looks like it may be an interesting read. As I write this some five years later, I'm still reading and referencing, discovering and applauding his words and his work. This is true magic, like a sunrise in the summer time or the shavings under your feet. The tiny purr of a kitten exploring through your workshop — inspiration is everywhere.

To you now, the reader, who I hope will draw from these pages some knowledge and inspiration of your own. In these fast-paced days of this our Global Village that constantly grows smaller each year through the high speed connections of time and of space. I welcome you to contact me, to discuss or address any questions or concerns you may have with these projects that I'm offering you here. Sharing ideas and designs from my heart and my hands with a hope that you too, will work them into pieces to call your own.

To Sandy, for not only being my own personal 'tech support' go-to guy, but for understanding and patiently putting our own projects on hold while I completed this work. Thanks.

And finally, to Douglas and Patrick, my brothers and constant creative companions; you are indeed both artists and educators alike and I'm proud to call you my friends.

This book is dedicated to my parents;

My father — who taught me the freedom of an honest day's wage and the strength in the working hand;

And to my mother — who always inspired me through the power of word and that of the mind.

Thanks and enjoy!

"Words are tools too blunt ..."

— Carlo Spinazzola 1970-2003

THE TIMBER FRAME PICTURED AT LEFT, AND THE QUOTE ABOVE ARE FROM one of my closest and dearest friends back home on Cape Breton Island. Carlo and I cut these timbers of Spruce and Fir together over a decade ago. He then milled them all by hand over the span of a few years, after transporting the heavy beams across the Island from North River to Big Pond.

An artist, woodworker, musician and painter — he forged my wedding band while I made my wife's in a metal forge in Cape Breton back in the summer of 2000 — a real jack of all trades, he was also a school teacher who taught kids in Northern Alberta until his death in 2003.

Carlo sadly ended his life while teaching up North and these massive sticks of timber, along with his words and his memory mean so much. Three years ago his family asked me if I wanted the timber that Carlo left stacked and unfinished on his dream land back on the North River ridge. At that time it had been sitting for years, and they worried it would begin to rot and become impossible to salvage. With no easy access to the top of the mountain and grown over by six years of alders and underbrush, brother Angelo and I cut our way through the bush to retrieve these precious beams.

What a view ... incredible.

Each one of these monoliths weighs 100 to 150 lbs. Two days of labor and a pretty emotional time in our life to say the least. I brought all of the beams back to my home (about a two-hour drive) on the other side of Cape Breton.

I promised myself and his brother to someday build Carlos' timber frame, or a variation of it, on the top of the mountain behind my home on Cape Breton — I won't get to it this year but hopefully someday — getting the timber up the hill and assembling it there will be another story altogether.

Rest in peace Brother. You are and always will be an inspiration.

CONTENTS

Wood and Why We Work It

TODAY, NOW MORE THAN EVER, WOODWORKERS AND artisans alike have unlimited options when building with, purchasing or using wood working tools. The cordless drill is as common today as the hammer was 50 years ago. Everyone knows and has seen home improvement programs on television and probably live within a few miles of a home center store selling everything from table saws and routers to dimensioned lumber and thickness planers.

The woodworker of the 21st century is the home handyman, the hobbyist and the weekend craftsman. Over the past decade or so things have been starting to change. Woodworkers are stepping back to an earlier time and using methods, traditions and hand tools borrowed from history books. Antique dealers and flea market peddlers watch as wide-eyed wood enthusiasts fight their way through the piles of bargains, looking for some special relic to bring home, tune up and dare I say — use? At the very least they will hang it on the woodshop wall or display it proudly in some custom-built showcase cabinet. Can you do 'real' work using these aged, traditional tools, sometimes older than your grandparents? Will the rust and the stains finally show their true limitations? The answers to these questions probably depend on the type of work you want to do; what are you expecting from your tools?

OPPOSITE 'Pretty Smooth...'
On the left, a Lie Nielsen No. 4 in Bronze.
On the right, a James Krenov custom Smoother.

HOW FINE IS FINE ANYWAY?

Hand tool users and aficionados are basking in a so-called revolution of hand tools and hand tool use. Flooding into our markets and overflowing the virtual shelves on the internet, specialty manufacturers are enjoying a renaissance of sorts. Today's modern woodworker and hobbyists are not looking to make a living from woodworking but simply want to find some satisfaction in working wood. The whole "do-it-yourself" campaign that allows relatively untrained hands to build pieces of furniture and household

accessories is alive and well. Our favorite magazines and television broadcasts, pod casts and instant satellite feeds, offer consumers easier, faster and better ways of creating a beautiful piece worthy enough to hand down to our grandchildren as family heirlooms.

Snake oil? You have to find out for yourself. Education is everywhere whether you choose to listen and learn it or not. One person will read this entire book and put it on a shelf somewhere, nothing gained and nothing lost. Another will take it and learn all that lies within; the written and un-written, can you read between the lines?

Be cautious when purchasing hand tools at the beginning of your own personal journey into woodworking. These new and improved versions are finely made

LEFT Re-claimed Elm; I bartered with a hold fast for this heavy slab … Thanks Mike!

BELOW Krenov smoothing plane on walnut.

crafting that perfect piece of furniture. Wishing only to use his hands and his hand tools; quietly shaping and sculpting.

A modern day Gepetto, creating thoughtful pieces of woodwork, worthy of true magic.

It's here in this place of grey uncertainty that we'll try to find some balance for a modern day hand tool-only woodshop. The reality of space confinements meeting the desire to work peacefully and safely; a place where oversized power tools are simply not an option and dust collection is merely the floor lying under your feet.

Looking into the past for answers of today and tomorrow, designs and desires, molded together into a true craft yet to be discovered; a secure and realistic pace at which to work. Not towards a simpler variation on design but more a finely jointed piece of furniture capable of longevity for years to come. These are very attainable goals in any small woodshop. A workbench, a tool cabinet and an assortment of hand tools, proudly kept out of harms way, finely tuned and ready to work with you. The masters hand trusting to lead; from rough milling through fine finishing, all will be addressed.

A refreshing change from the noise and the dust, accidents are from your hands alone. What follows are the tales and techniques to walk through a door and into a space where you too can create these pieces out of wood. A physical, mental and spiritual challenge, when patience will be virtuous and the rewards immeasurable. Not just a fine furniture destination but a journey through woodcraft indeed.

Let's put the Art back into the Craft. Welcome.

and tuned right out of the box. Ready to work with you, they will actually bring your woodworking to another level indeed. However, they don't come cheap. Cheap tools are just that ... cheap!

You can use older, refurbished hand tools, but believe me when I say; when it comes to quality tools, you truly get what you pay for. I have met many men and women who would love to do some form of woodwork but simply do not have the real estate to house a shop full of power tools. The dust and noise, the dangers and well, the fear; these are real things that need to be addressed. If you were to price out a basic woodshop equipped with power tools and compare it to a workshop only using hand tools, the hand tool shop owner may still have a few dollars left in the bank for purchasing actual lumber. Wood

can be expensive and money doesn't grow on trees.

Enter the hand tool woodshop. People can easily spend small fortunes on the new fandangled handsaws and reissued hand planes. Imported chisels from foreign shores where they're still being made to serve a practical purpose and not for the enjoyment or entertainment of the amateur woodworker.

There is a place for these tools, working towards a reachable level of fine workmanship in the home or hobby woodshop. A work space may be only a small room in a condo, rising out of a skyline 50 stories above the street. No trees for miles, an asphalt landscape, where to find anything handcrafted would be next to impossible. Even here, in this cold space of steel and cement, the woodworker hides, dreaming of

CHAPTER ONE

Essentials

BEFORE WE GET INTO THE WHOLE 'WHICH HAND tools are absolutely necessary debate' the success you'll find while using this book will depend on where you set up your work space. We'll address some of the fundamentals involved with setting up a woodshop, from tool storage to workbenches, wood racks and saw horses.

To give a point of reference, my shop in Cape Breton was an old 20' by 20' one car garage. I basically gutted it and used this relatively small space to set up my first wood shop. Keeping in mind that in my first shop I had things like a table saw, band saw, jointer, planer, router table, wood stove, wood racks, assembly area and of course a workbench. Not to mention things like cat food and kitty litter, extra firewood piled in the corner, paint cans, cordless drills and circular saws. Chop saws and random orbital sanders littered old shelves I acquired when someone was throwing them out. Vacuums and dark corners full of cob webs with unused items I either forgot I had or simply never needed in the first place. A lot of noise and a lot of dust, this shop had issues like inadequate power, insufficient lighting and optimum-use floor space.

OPPOSITE **Before any wood shavings can fall, a successful project begins here, between the lines.**

HAND TOOL EPIPHANY

At some point in my wood working endeavors I decided to build a 'Bench Room' onto the existing workshops' footprint. I blew-out the back wall on a fine summer's afternoon and added a 12' × 16' space across the back. I decided this new room would become my 'Hand Tool Haven'; a work space that would keep me focused and content; inspired and comfortably safe while working with wood.

A conscious decision was made to keep this area free of power tools, noise and dust; to store my hand tools in a proper tool cabinet, a wood rack for dry lumber, a saw bench and of course my workbenches. I actually have two benches but that's another story I'll save for later. I installed three big windows in the new bench room, some adequate overhead lighting and painted the walls an egg shell white. A kind of 'cottage comfort' with lots of natural lighting, this bright and clean space became my perfect retreat; 'Workbench Zen' was scribbled across the wall just above

my Bench. I hung art work and old tools in areas around the room, inspirational pieces of literature as well as small artifacts from my past. People that came to visit thought of this space as a kind of studio in waiting, a wood-shop Nirvana that bred a slower pace where one could work and design in a relaxed and calming atmosphere. This small 12' × 16' room is what we're going to try to recreate; a work space that welcomes you in and breeds productive thoughts. If you live in an area that already has such a space, great;

if you have a garage or basement, a shed in the yard, then this will work as well. Even if you live in a small apartment, 50 stories in the air, then perhaps a spare bedroom could be adequate. One of the great parts of using hand tools to build furniture is that it doesn't require a whole lot of room; it doesn't spew out toxins and nasty by-products. Noise and air pollution are kept to almost nothing, so you're neighbors shouldn't be banging on the walls or complaining about the dust creeping out from under your door.

NOW, ON TO THE TALE OF THE TWO BENCHES...

Once I decided to add the extra room to my work shop back in Cape Breton, I also decided I needed a new workbench. My initial thought was to build one, I mean that's the way it's supposed to work isn't it? I read all I could and browsed endless websites searching for the perfect design that could work for me and the work that I do. This point is so important yet somehow forgotten when designing ones own bench. What kind of work do you do? How much surface area do you require? How often or what style vises would I use? Before you go and start building from some

ABOVE **Bench room in my first shop, Cape Breton Island, 2007.**

LEFT **Tool cabinet.**

Fully restored 1903 Millers Falls Hand drill.

ing, I also enjoyed and occasionally would get paid for building wooden boats back on the coast.)

So I start building the ordered boat for my customer and again, ring-ring ... someone else wants a built-in hutch for their dining room area. It was starting to look like my bench would have to wait a while. Then, one day not too long after, while surfing on the internet, I stumbled over a company that was selling European made, cabinet-maker workbenches for a price I couldn't refuse. I decided better to buy one than to keep the paying customer waiting while I tried to find the time to build one. I ordered it and waited patiently for three weeks for it to arrive. I was like a kid on Christmas morning when the delivery truck pulled up my driveway; tearing open cardboard to find a slightly damaged Bench top and a few missing pieces. Oh well, not the end of the world I thought. I'd simply phone the company and tell them of the issues. The gentleman representing the company apologized immediately for the inconvenience and said a replacement bench would be shipped out ASAP. So I re-packaged up the damaged bench and waited two more weeks. When the new bench finally arrived I did the whole inspection for any bruises; none, great. I assembled it and went on like everything was normal. Another week had passed and the damaged bench was still there, eating up valuable floor space in my never-large-enough shop. I placed a call again to the company and was told the workbench would be picked-up. Another week goes by and the telephone rings again.

"Hello Tom, we've decided to 'abandon' the bench due to the costs of shipping it back. You're free to do with it what you see fit."

Well, isn't that something, a sweet deal just got a little bit sweet-

old design posted somewhere, think about what it is that you're expecting from the bench.

So there I was, finally decided on a bench style that I felt would suit my work and Wham! The telephone rings and someone wants me to build them a 12' traditional-style wooden boat. (Besides building furniture and writing about wood worker; I mean where else could you get two-for-one workbenches? I did have to make some repairs but still get a lot of use out of the damaged bench. Having the extra work surface is great for my sharpening station as well as a space to lay out extra components while working. Who could argue with that? So, my point here? Find a workbench you're happy with and either build it yourself or buy one already manufactured.

My advice would be to read- *Workbenches: From Design & Theory to Construction & Use* by Christopher Schwarz. This will cover everything you'll ever need to know on the subject of workbenches.

THE LAST TOOLS YOU'LL EVER NEED?

Once you've laid claim to a shop space and have addressed the whole workbench issue, we'll move on to compiling a list of the essential hand tools you'll need to build furniture. The last tools you'll ever need? Probably not, but it should prove to be a real good starting point. To be frank, hand tools are incredibly addictive and while you can perform multiple tasks on a certain tool; it's nice to have the freedom some specialty tools offer to perform specific tasks and operations.

First off I'd like to address the furniture building procedures I see as being somewhat different from building furniture using power tools. We're trained from an early age of using shop tools that repetition is a benefit when exercised in building and craft work. This is true when doing multiple techniques, lumping stages of an operation together into recurring junctions in order to speed things up or perhaps to try to eliminate error.

Example: Performing repeated tasks on the table saw. At the beginning stages of building a small table, one may do all of the ripping

cuts on the table saw for all of the pieces of the entire project. Then we tend to move on to perhaps the cross-cut saw and again follow this systematic method. It's indeed a direct descendant of the assembly line way of thinking and working. Do all of one precise task and then, move on and carry out the next.

When working with hand tools I really don't see the benefit in this other than perhaps the physical workout you may obtain. Sure you'll get better at a certain skill but this is not practice time. Practice on scrap wood before you get into building a piece of furniture. What seems to work the best for me is choosing a logical starting point, such as a tables legs; take this element and

Some oldies and goodies; Two of these classic braces are my daily users and the other two? Well, let's just say they're sort of hanging around...

work through the beginning stages of preparation until it's close to a finished state, smooth and ready for joinery; then take the next logical piece and do the same. Take the part rough milled, rip it, cross cut it and then go back and do the same to the next. After the sawing stages you could plane the pieces down. Get them all ready for the joinery stage; then go back and bring the next piece to the same point. Do all of the sawing and planing for the entire project over a day or two and then, when everything is at that point; you can start thinking about the joinery. Keep in mind these are only guidelines and suggestions; each piece you build may present its own unique ways of procedure. Perhaps you'll need to cut everything at once and then move on to another stage. Maybe you need all of the planing practice you can get and will put all of the planing operations together. Work in a way that's best for you but do read and try to understand the reasoning behind the suggestions I offer you here. Then, once you see there is a different way of doing things or at least one other point of view, close the book and make up your own mind. Think about the processes you'll need to work through. Think about the piece you're making and the wood you'll be using. Think about the reality of multiple components, gluing up in stages, do you even have enough clamps? Where will you put the wood shavings?

The hand tool list on the following pages is merely a starting point. You may end up using some, all or more tools than I'll mention here in the text. The list I've compiled represents the tools I've used in building the pieces described within these pages. There are so many new and exciting hand tool manufacturers popping up all over the marketplace it can be a little intimidating to choose. Which plane is better? How does that one feel? Do I really need to spend that much? I'm not going to recommend any specific brand or manufacturer here, however I will include a Resource Section at the back of the book with some of the more popular manufacturers and distributors I've used and can honestly recommend to you.

I don't see anything wrong with using old or antique tools either, in a lot of cases these 'oldies but goodies' are far superior than most off-the-shelf, big-box variety hand tools

Lay-out tools.

available today. But buyers beware — keep a keen eye when purchasing old tools. Tuning up antiques to use as daily workers can be a challenge and will take some time and some sweat. Some of the flea market treasures turn out to be better left on the flea market shelf however, every once in awhile a real gem comes along and with little or no effort you can have yourself a finely tuned, woodworking antique.

I've also noticed a few individuals lately, offering old-refurbished tools to users. These are top notch re-builds done by professionals. I recently purchased a fully restored Millers Falls hand drill No. 1. This drill was manufactured in 1903 and fully restored by Wiktor Kuc in 2008. That's 105 years in the making! He does amazing restoration work and I feel lucky to own such a masterful example of tool making and renovation.

There is something nice about using a tool built in an age when hand tools were common place in the home woodshop. That said there's also something quite nice about a brand-spanking new, cutting edge hand tool fresh out of the box, and ready to work!

I guess the best way to say it is this: If you want to do serious hand tool work then the reality is you need to use serious hand tools. Be it a finely tuned classic or a brand new, high end boutique variety, keeping your tools well tuned, properly set-up and maintained with razor sharp edges means all of the difference in working wood.

LAY-OUT TOOLS:

When you take that first piece of lumber down from your wood rack the first tool you'll reach for is a lay-out tool. These are essentials, get all of them.

- Measuring Tape at least 10' long
- 24" steel rule (I have the centre-finding variety which comes in real handy)
- 6" Steel Rule
- Combination square
- 1 or 2 engineer squares
- 2 sets of Dividers
- Dovetail marker or sliding bevel gauge
- Marking Gauge
- Marking Knife
- Awl
- Winding Sticks
  (Specs on how to make your own winding sticks in Chapter Four.)

CUTTING TOOLS

After you select your lumber for a project; the first step is going to be cross-cutting it into more manageable sizes followed usually by ripping and surfacing. The joinery saws listed are again only a suggestion; these are the tools I have in my own shop and the models I've used to build the pieces here. I think they represent a good starting point for the beginner wood worker.

Hand Saws

- Cross Cut Panel saw
- Rip Panel saw
- Dovetail Saw
- Fret Saw (For removing the waste between dovetails)
- Bow saw for cutting curves and/ or removing dovetail waste
- 2 Larger scale Tenon Saws one cross-cut and the other filed rip for cutting joinery

The Push and the Pull of It …
Western vs. Japanese-style Handsaws

I've read a lot on the topic and have listened to many good debates regarding the matter of Western vs. Japanese style hand saws. The argument of pushing and pulling, blades of grass

and fingertips; brittle teeth and North American hard woods too dense for the weaker, foreign tooth style …

Sounds a little like an automotive commercial doesn't it?

Well, I'm from the shores where things work by working. Simple enough right?

Not quite the 'If it's not broke don't fix it' bit, but if something is working then work it! Early on while practicing my hand tool skills building traditional style wooden boats, I would order relatively inexpensive, Japanese style saws through mail order catalogues. These hand saws were razor sharp and took the daily boat shop abuses, from cutting the ends of hard white oak planks to sawing fine dovetails in eastern maple. I never did find any issues with teeth breaking or saws binding … remember, when using these fragile hand tools that you will only bind a saw when you try to use your muscles instead of your mind. Use your head and let the saw do the sawing! That is what it was designed to do.

Now woodworkers who grew up using Western style push saws may think this cutting on the pull stroke for the birds. Indeed!

A few of the hand saws in my work shop.

With that I'll say get your Western style saws finely tuned or spend the money and purchase both a fine cross-cut and a rip saw. The quality available today in North American handsaws is astonishing. Within an arms reach from my workbench I have three 'turbocharged', garage sale-antique variety hand saws that will deal with any of the ripping or cross-cutting tasks from the projects in this book.

I also have a nest of different back-saws all ready to work as well. They're all Western style; hanging, waiting along side of my three Japanese style saws.

Do I have a preference? No, not really. The finely shaped hardwood handles and brass screws on the Western style saws are certainly nicer to look at than the rather plain bamboo-like softwood on the Japanese pull saws; but both styles find their way into my hands all of the time. Flush cuts and fast trims, super small pieces; I always reach for the pull saws. Dovetails and tenons, long rips and thick cross-cuts it's the push stroke, the Western

style. There is a place in the workshop for both but for the beginner I'd say try them all. Buy an inexpensive, decent quality Ryoba saw; this is the one with both the rip tooth and cross-cut pattern; let the saw do the sawing and you do your best not to force it. Then get a dedicated dovetail saw; a good one. Look closely at the pictures through the book and see the one I use. You won't be disappointed. Then, watch around at flea markets and garage sales, find some old panel saw that someone is 'giving away' then find a reputable saw sharpener or restorer and have them overhaul it.

Mark Harrell (www.technoprimitives.com) is someone I can honestly say takes a real pride in this area. He re-worked the magic into three old 'beaters' I purchased for $15.00 — that was for all three! Without sounding too much like an advertisement, they truly are priceless, at least to me and my work. Trust your own judgment and use what works for you. Let the politicians argue over the whole East vs. West debate.

HAND PLANES
Scrub Plane
To begin. I should start by saying if you purchase pre-dimensioned wood (surface-planed on two sides with at least one edge jointed), then you probably won't need to go out and get a scrub plane. If however you buy rough milled lumber, then the scrub plane will be the first tool you reach for. The Veritas plane (pictured in the photo above), has served me well for the past few years.

Jointer or Fore Plane
Again taking into account the scale of the work you'll be doing buying a jointer plane or a fore or Jack plane should be next on your list. The jointer is a perfect tool for leveling

A good start- Left to right: Lie-Nielsen No. 4 smoothing plane in Bronze, a Veritas Scrub plane, a Lie-Nielsen 5½ Jack plane and finally a Lie-Nielsen 102, low-angle block plane. This small plane is in my hand on a daily basis.

large surfaces and wide timbers. If you work more with smaller sized pieces you could easily get away with a Jack plane. To joint, surface, smooth and shoot I suppose that's the reason it's referred to as a 'Jack' (of all trades) plane.

Smoothing Plane
After your stock is flat and square you'll need to go over the entire surface again with a smoothing plane. There are a staggering number of options available to the woodworker today so I'll recommend you go out and try a few. I use an old, pre-world war one Stanley with corrugated sole and the pictured Lie-Nielsen

ABOVE **A good joinery combination. At left the Veritas small plough plane and at right the Lie-Nielsen skew block. Since writing this I've noticed Lie-Nielsen is now offering a tongue and groove plane; this may be something to consider … yes I know I have a hand plane problem; but at least I can admit it!**

RIGHT **Veritas small router plane and, Lie-Nielsen side rabbet planes.**

in bronze. The extra weight of the bronze really helps to keep it moving.

Low-Angle Block Plane
For chamfering edges, dealing with end grain or shaping tables legs, the low-angle block plane is a must.

SPECIAL-PURPOSE PLANES
Plough Plane
For cutting grooves and dadoes this is an essential joinery tool. This newer metal variety has an easy-to-use depth stop, a solid fence to register your work and has five different blade size options. A well made tool by Veritas.

140 Skew Block Plane and/or Rabbet Plane
Again for cutting joinery such as a rabbet in the side of a panel these planes are the answer. Usually available in both a left- and right-hand version, I decided to purchase one of each.

Large and /or Small Router Planes
A router plane is not the first special purpose plane I'd get but there's nothing like it for cutting recesses to pre-determined depths or cleaning out a long groove.

Side Rabbet Planes
Not an essential but again, nice to have; especially if you're using a router plane a lot. I tend to make a few passes with the router and then a light pass with a side rabbet. People tend to think of these small planes as something to reach for when you've made an error during lay-out and need to widen a groove or rabbet. I've set mine up to take fine shavings and can clean the inside edges of a groove quite easily with this tool.

OPPOSITE **A collection of spoke shaves in the tool cabinet.**

ABOVE **The grouping of chisels pictured is only part of my collection; it is however a very capable 'kit' adequate to handle the scope of the projects in this book. From right to left: Sorby Boxwood-Handled Paring Chisels, Veritas Detail chisel set, Henry Taylor Swan neck chisel, Lie-Nielsen Mortising chisels, Hirsch Firmer Chisels, Japanese style dovetail and large bench chisels and finally a pair of Firmer Gouges.**

Spokeshaves

I recommend you purchase a Flat bottom spoke shave as soon as you can, the wooden body type ones are fine and getting nicer all of the time, however I still like using the new style, metal body products on the market today. A Round Bottom Spoke shave will also come in handy.

Scrapers

You can't say enough about the importance of scrapers in the wood shop. Cabinet scrapers and scraping planes, card scrapers a must. When every tool fails you and that wild grained wood is getting closer and closer to the fire wood pile, the cabinet scraper can be a savior in taming the tear-out. An assortment of card scrapers is essential.

Knives

A couple of decent knives will be a benefit to the hand tool user as well. A marking knife is obvious but also a carving knife is handy for small details and general cutting. I have a small assortment of hand made knives by Paul Beebe, a Canadian knife maker. They come in handy for marking out fine dovetails with extremely thin pins where my regular marking knife would be too wide.

CHISELS

A quality set of bench chisels in the $1/4$" up to 1" range is a must have.

For 'specialty type' chisels you can probably do without full sets; maybe start of with a couple of sizes, $1/4$" and $1/2$" perhaps a $3/8$" would be a safe bet and work your way from there.

Mortising Chisels/Dovetail Chisels

I'll also recommend you have at least one small chisel, in the $1/8$" range for getting into those tight spots while fitting joints. A quality set of 'detail chisels' are a real nice item to own; I have a beautiful set designed by cabinet maker, Yeung Chan and can say I use them every day.

Lastly, at the other end of the chisel inventory spectrum is one large chisel, maybe in the $1 1/2$" to 2" width range. This will become a real work horse around the shop.

MAKING HOLES

When it comes to hand drills and braces, flea market tools and antique dealers are the way to go. You can find piles of quality braces barely used for the better part of fifty years. They may have a little rust but a simple cleaning and some light machine oil is all it takes to bring them back to working order.

Hand drills, the egg beater type, are also creeping back into the markets. I've already mentioned my old Millers Falls — a real pleasure to use and once you've tried one you'll never reach for the cordless again.

Drilling tools.

The control and ease of these drills is incredible; fine, precise work on a smaller scale, (pre-drilling holes for hardware) is easy and effortless.

Also useful are Auger Gimlets. A starter hole for finish nails or pre-drilling holes for screws in hardwood, these old school hand drills excel. They are still manufactured and are a joy to use. Your kit will be better off with a set ranging in size from a #2 up to a #9.

> *"To catch gentle shavings, as they fall from your hand planes".*

WHERE TWO PLANES MEET
Some Thoughts on Sharpening

The best hand tool in the world is worthless in the hands of the woodworker who doesn't know how to sharpen it.

What is sharp? Where two planes meet. That tiny island almost invisible to the eye, this is the land of sharpness. Read about it, practice it and then strive to master what ever technique you decide works best for you. There are so many methods and jigs on the market today, grinders and guides, stones and abrasives. In properly trained hands all of them have the potential to work, just pick one or two and go at it. Common sense can also help, if you'll be working in an unheated shop as I started in back in Cape Breton, then water stones probably

won't do the job, maybe sand paper on glass would be a practical solution? Speak to fellow woodworkers and research the forums on line, read all you can on the topic or find a class or workshop somewhere. You'll never run out of literature, methods or techniques and you're tools will never be too sharp!

Another point to consider (no pun intended) are jigs and sharpening guides; they can help you learn the methods and enable you to consistently sharpen and re-sharpen an edge. My advice to you is to try them.

I've wandered to and fro', sharpening jigs and honing guides to free hand techniques and mere luck. One month I'd use a jig and then the next I'd try the free hand approach. I would keep going back and forth trying to learn a proper

Sharpening a plane iron with adhesive backed sandpaper on safety glass with a honing guide.

system while discovering for myself what methods worked for me and why. These days it seems I've come to rely on my honing guides and water stones except when I'm smack dab in the middle of some crucial step and must admit, I'll run over and 'free hand' a polish on the 8000 grit stone. The guides take a few more seconds to set up but they're usually worth the extra effort. I know that when I use them properly, they're dependable and accurate; it's usually only the 'hassle' of learning the dance that keeps beginners away from using water stones. Messy ... yeah, sure they are. But once you get yourself around that and find

Grain maps — a good test of a sharp tool.

your way into a routine, they'll bring you closer to that space on the edge we're so desperately seeking.

Some times my free hand techniques aren't so reliable; those early winter mornings after a 'few' the night before ... hey, we're all human and hands can sometimes have a mind or at least a wave of they're own. On those chilly days in the middle of a long Canadian winter I can use all of the help I can get.

To think back to the initial steps I took into sharpening; I probably had my first set of knock-about chisels for three years before it ever even occurred to me to sharpen them! A kind of evolution people and tools go through when they first meet, say in the isle of a big box store on a busy weekend of deconstruction and renovation with friends or fam-

ily. "Hey cousin, you want to come over on Saturday and help me build a new deck; it is coming onto barbe-cue season you know." I think many woodworkers first get introduced to the love of working wood this way; through assisting friends with projects or perhaps a renovation of your own. Almost sounds roman-tic doesn't it, except that this first courting can sometimes devolve from new shiny chisels to old dull screwdrivers. I can remember pry-ing old roofing tar off of asphalt shingles and then busting out rough grooves in some softwood 2 × 4's; wet, crooked and just as cheap as the tools I was using. These are the realities of finding your way into the fold ... this was 20 years ago and I'm happy to say I've found my way through the fog ... well almost.

I'm always learning and trying new techniques. I found one that works for me but we all should continue to set new goals for ourselves, reaching new levels and trying new methods and ideas. Sharpening as well as working procedures need to be chal-lenged, developed and reconsidered again and again, over and over. I try to keep it simple but my shop now has a couple of honing guides, some water stones and still the sand paper on glass and I continue to discover each one has merits.

Honing Guides
Jigs work, use them!

Is it really that simple? It certain-ly can be; I first purchased a narrow wheel style honing guide years ago after I started sharpening using oil stones. I didn't quite get to the part of the story where you should keep these stones dead flat but that fortunately came later. I picked up one of those inexpensive, combination grit oil stones at the local hardware store and would use it every once in a while with this small honing guide. No cambered edges or micro-bevels, just maintaining the angled factory edge on my cheaply manufactured hand tools and trying my best not to hurt myself. Inconsistent results to say the least. I still didn't know what a really sharp edge looked or performed like so there wasn't really any frustration at this point; mostly ignorant bliss and a complete unawareness of the possibilities ahead when using finely maintained high-quality hand tools.

I can't now remember when I first learned that a sharpened edge is the perfect combination of TWO flat surfaces! Ahhh ... the bevel side and the flat back side of a chisel or plane iron. Makes sense. Where two planes meet, right?

What a difference this made, the concept of flattening the back of an iron instantly amplified the problems I had with un-flat sharpening surfaces. The oil stones I had been using were immediately transformed into paper weights. Fortunately, I did some research and found out about water stones. This seemed like my best solution until I read somewhere else about water stones freezing and cracking. Foiled again in the wood stove heated woodshop I continued on down the learning curve until I discovered the system of safety glass and micro-abrasives. Lee Valley Tools offered the supplies and I finally started to get somewhere. This would have been in conjunction with learning the skills in proper hand tool set up and flattening the soles of my hand planes. Setting up these new tools

and the work that is required on most hand tools is an art in itself; even straight out of a box, fresh from the manufacturer. Needless to say this was also before I discovered places like Lie Nielsen Toolworks where you can easily take a tool, fresh out of its packing material and start working with it. More honing can always help but really, most high end tool manufacturers are making our lives in the woodshop easier and more enjoyable with less time worrying about the quality of the hand tool and more time thinking about the furniture you'll be creating with them.

So back in the unheated boat shop all those years ago, I began using a three grit sandpaper approach as you would with most sharpening systems, a coarse, medium and to finish, a polishing grit. This method also used a small drop of light oil to help build up a slurry on the paper surface; another important factor in sharpening. The

sandpaper on glass worked although I was frequently frustrated with paper tearing and inconsistent wearing of the surface grit.

I also noticed around this time (while ordering my sharpening supplies through the mail) that Veritas offered a kind of super-charged honing guide called the Mk. II. This made things much easier for me and introduced yet another new concept in the sharpening realm; the micro-bevel as well as a back bevel. These unfamiliar terminologies opened up a real can of worms. Why hone, polish and sharpen entire surfaces when we could manipulate the angle of a cutting tool while sharpening and create smaller surfaces that would not only be easier to re-sharpen and hone but be a much faster procedure as well.

Think about the large flat back side of a cutting iron; that initial time when you spent those long hours honing away on your finest grit adhesives; working up a mir-

Honing guides are your friends!

ror like finish, making sure that at minimum this final ¼" where the flat meets the bevel is perfectly free from the manufacturer's marks and deeper scratches showing through. If we back up a step we would have began on a coarse to medium stone, back and forth making sure we've taken the proper steps to insure the sharpening medium we're using is truly flat.

This can be done with ease with sandpaper on a flat surface like the safety glass I mentioned or get a granite off cut from a home center or home center building store. Maybe the top of the table saw if you have one nearby. Basically a flat surface and a sheet of 220 grit sandpaper, mark the stone you're using in pencil lines and give them a little rub together. Have a look and see how the stone is wearing. If you notice the pencil lines are still there in the center then you have a hollow, if they're still on the edges then

you have a hump. Keep scribbling away and checking the reference until you know the stones are dead flat. You obviously don't need to do this if you're dealing with sandpaper on glass but try to maintain a consistent wear on the paper. If you notice the middle of the sheet wearing faster than the edges it's time to replace it with some new stock.

Now back to these altered angles and back beveled backs. I'm starting to sound like Dr. Seuss but you'll soon get used to the terminology. We are no longer required to polish the entire working surfaces both on the bevel side as well as the flat side. When I first get a new tool I still go through my ritual of flattening and honing the back, from a 1000 grit stone up to an 8000 grit. I'll spend an hour and clear my mind, enjoy the process and keep checking my stones for flat. Remember that step! Before, during and after each sharpening session; it's easy to bypass it

With just a few tools, it's fairly easy to keep your blades sharp, and ready to work.

and the result will be hollows and rounds all over the surface; almost defeating yourself before you begin, so to speak. The same is true for the angled, cutting surfaces of an iron as well; why try to hone the entire bevel when we can simply polish the tiniest leading edge? A micro-bevel if you will.

In more recent years, I've discovered the sharpening methods used and taught by David Charlesworth, a master craftsman, cabinetmaker and teacher in England; David's method of using a thin metal rule to hold up one side of the cutting iron while you're honing the back is truly unique, almost startling in simplicity but genius in practice. The 'ruler trick' as most people refer to it is essentially creating a shelf or wedge with the rule on one side of the water stone while the plane iron lays across it and sits angled to the surface while you hone the back on the opposite side of the stone. You're no longer flattening the entire back side of the iron but merely a small leading edge where the business occurs. This really makes a ton of sense but again, it's good practice to check the entire surface for bumps and render them flat with a course to medium stone prior to the ruler trick. This procedure will also be performed after you've addressed the bevel side in daily usage.

When I moved from Cape Breton, to Toronto and the luxury of a heated basement workspace, one of the first things I purchased were water stones. I went with the Norton brand in a 1000, 1000/4000

grit combo and finally the 8000 polishing stone. I've since added a 220 grit stone to my sharpening arsenal for really removing metal in a hurry or for those times when I notice a small chip in an edge. I still use my Mk. II honing guide for irons that require a straight cutting edge from one side of the iron across to the other or for any of my skewed chisels or irons.

The Veritas line comes with some helpful accessories to add still other dimensions to your sharpening routine. Learning the Charlesworth techniques have again opened up new avenues to practice and pursue. This new idea and concept of cambered edges or rounded blades; essentially what

we're trying to do when sharpening a cambered edge is basically rolling off the sharp outside corners of the iron so while hand planing we're not left with 'plane tracks' in the wood. Some people imagine that the cambered edge looks something like a scrub plane blade; this is not accurate. The camber is a much gentler curve almost invisible to the eye. These tracks that often creep up and out of the wood grain when we use a straight blade in our hand planes are removed during the following stages of smoothing the surface. From one pass of a plane to the next without the iron corners rounded over we're going to have difficulties attaining an acceptable finished surface. I do not camber my jointing plane, (the straight edge is needed when edge jointing boards) my special purpose planes like a plough, shoulder or rabbet nor do I round over any of my chisels; just my smoothing planes, my Jacks and finally my block planes. I recommend any of the Charlesworth literature or videos for a much more detailed look into this cambered blade concept.

I still use my narrow wheel honing guide for all of the curved blades and as mentioned the Mk. II for skewed and un-cambered irons.

I've recently noticed high end ceramic stones being offered and used by top wood workers in the public eye. They seem like another step closer in achieving a perfectly flat and sharpened hand tool edge (which I should mention is absolutely unattainable) but what you should strive for is a very attainable and suitable place in this sharpening zone. The closest tolerances you can get to without going completely mad! You're work will thank you, your tools will perform as they were intended and the joys of working wood will be that much the greater. Take your time.

The Ruler Trick adds a simple back bevel that makes sharpening even quicker.

CHAPTER TWO

Workbench Appliances

WHEN STARTING INTO THE DAY-TO-DAY WORKINGS IN A hand tool shop we can sometimes get lost in the methods of work. Time can be wasted considering the how's and the why's when we could be better spending our time working wood.

There are three benchtop 'appliances' that are simple to make, easy to use and will save you a lot of time and effort in your woodworking. To begin we'll look at the bench hook, a straight forward bench top saver that will come in handy when planning thin stock.

OPPOSITE **Shooting an edge with a Lie-Nielsen #5^1/$_2$.**

The bench hook.

Planing thin material with narrow fence acting as a plane stop.

THE BENCH HOOK

This straightforward design is quick and easy to build. I used some ³/₄" Baltic Birch plywood for the main table as well as the front lower hook. The top fence is a thin piece of white oak. I used plywood for the top in this newer version because not only is it a very stable product, it will be a little gentler on tool edges than medium density fiberboard.

The fence is kept as thin as possible; this comes in handy as a plane stop when working on thin materials. I'll also use this surface for any small chopping, paring or general chisel work.

Begin by cutting the plywood 12"-wide × 16"-long; make sure to use good quality stuff that has at least one good side. The front hook is also cut from the ³/₄" plywood; I cut this one to 1" × 12" and then glued and screwed it to the lower front edge. For the top fence I used a piece of white oak I had left over from a project and dimensioned it to 2"-wide, 12"-long and just under ¼" in thickness. This is held about 1" from the edge and gets carefully squared up, glued and clamped

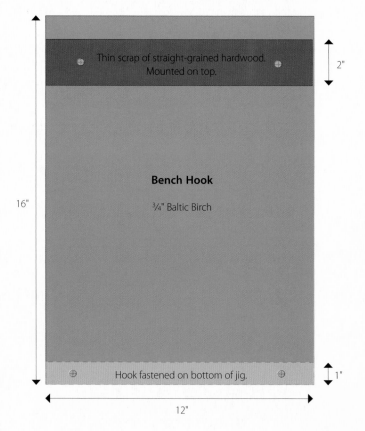

Thin scrap of straight-grained hardwood. Mounted on top.

2"

16"

Bench Hook

³/₄" Baltic Birch

Hook fastened on bottom of jig.

1"

12"

overnight. You can add some small nails for some added strength but I never have and the glue has held on so far. (Knock on wood.)

I'll generally leave this jig sitting on my bench top most of the time. For small lay-outs, chiseling or any-

time I just want to quickly hold a small piece of stock in place while I clean up the faces, this simple design does a great job holding things in place or at the very least, keeping your workbench free of any chisel marks.

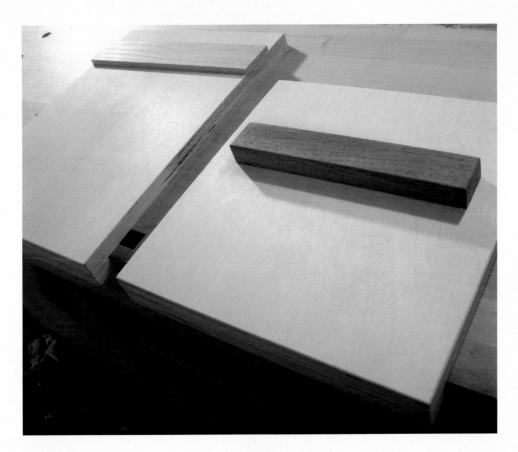

LEFT Miter hook with heavy quarter-sawn walnut fence next to my bench hook. Once you make these simple jigs you'll wonder how you ever got along without them.

BELOW Work piece on the front of the fence being cut on the push stroke with a western style handsaw.

THE MITER HOOK

The miter hook is another benchtop appliance and is constructed following the same design as the bench hook. Beginning with a ³⁄₄" piece of suitable hardboard, cut a piece 12"-wide by 12"-long. On the lower front edge, attach a 1" × 12" strip to establish the 'hook'. From here you'll need an appropriate piece of hardwood in the 1"- to 1¹⁄₄"-thickness. I had a nice straight grained piece of quarter sawn walnut that I cut to 10" long. The 2" difference in width is purposeful; once attached it will leave a 1" gap on either side of your miter hook against which you can register your saw blade when making cuts. If you only use a Western style saw, which cuts on the push stroke, then you can attach the fence relatively close to the end of the main body, however if you're like me and use both Western and Japanese style saws, then attach the fence further away from the far end of the board.

This will enable you to place stock being cut on the far side when using a Japanese style saw, (which cuts on the pull stroke), making your cuts safe and reliable.

Keep your work in place while making the cut. When constructing this jig I usually wait until the fence is firmly glued and let stand to dry overnight and then make my reference cuts in the fence. For my first miter hook, I cut a left handed 45° kerf about an inch off of center, a center line kerf and then on the right hand side another 45° cut. This worked out quite well and I happily used this hook for a few years.

Not too long ago I was rummaging through some old tools at a garage sale in my neighborhood and I came across a great old miter box manufactured by Stanley. The elderly gentleman was only asking ten dollars for this fine old relic. I snapped it up and took it home and after a bit of cleaning, painting and oiling, this thing is as good as new. If you're lucky enough to come across one then by all means get it and use it ... you won't regret

it. Since buying the old Stanley I've since made myself a new miter hook and this time it only has the square cuts registered in the fence. I figure I'll use the old Stanley for my miter cuts and the miter hook for making straight square cuts.

Bench top clutter on a typical, busy work day. Notice my first, well worn miter hook in the foreground with its mitered kerfs along side of the center cut. Just beyond it on the bench top is my shooting board.

THE SHOOTING BOARD

The shooting board or 'chute' board is another one of these bench top appliances that you really shouldn't be without. When I walk into a woodshop without one I'm astonished — why on earth wouldn't you take an hour or two at best and with a small amount of wood and off-cuts make yourself one?

The woodworker who hasn't yet made themselves an honest shooting board simply doesn't realize the benefits and ease that comes with having this practical bench-top jig.

My first shooting board was made from ¾" medium density fiberboard (MDF) with a quarter-sawn white oak fence. It has served me quite well for years. Until

TOP **The first shooting board I made a few years back out of MDF with a quarter sawn White Oak fence. I'm using it here with my more than adequate and quite capable 5½ Bench plane.**

BOTTOM **After purchasing a dedicated iron miter plane from Lie-Nielsen Tool Works I redesigned my shooting board. My newest and current 'chute' design is shown here.**

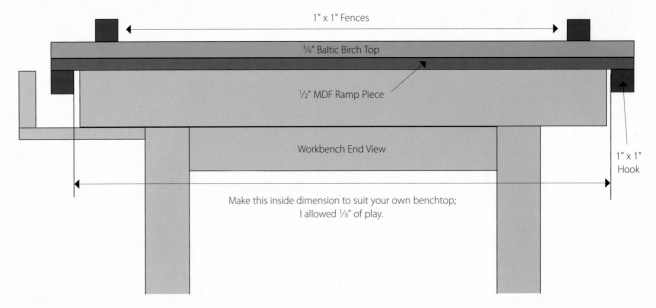

1" x 1" Fences

¾" Baltic Birch Top

½" MDF Ramp Piece

Workbench End View

1" x 1"
Hook

Make this inside dimension to suit your own benchtop;
I allowed ⅛" of play.

recently, I'd always used a No. 5½ bench plane to do my shooting. The purchase of a dedicated 'shooter', the Lie-Nielsen No. 9 iron miter plane has changed that. This is one serious hand plane! It's modeled after the old original Stanley No. 9 and as a devoted shooting plane you can't go wrong. One of the many fine features of this hand plane is it can be used on the left or right side of the board. Given this fact I decided to build myself a new and improved shooting board to compliment the new No. 9.

The plans here are dimensioned for my current workbench so before you get started building your own, take note and adjust to suit your own bench top.

One handy feature I find with this design is while in my basement workshop, where space is quite limited, I can stand on either side of the workbench and without picking up or altering the 'chute' in any way, be able to work with it comfortably from one side to another.

To begin construction, I used some ¾" Baltic Birch for the shooting table; this is fastened down to a ½" piece of MDF by way of glue and screws up through the bottom. The MDF is the same overall length as the plywood but is made wider to create the 'ramp' your shooting plane will ride on. Seeing as the No. 9 can easily be used left- or right-handed, and I wanted to use the jig from both sides of the bench,

I decided to incorporate a double ramp to accommodate this feature. Again I attached a 1" fence to the front, underside of the MDF, however where this appliance differs from most I've seen is here: on the front underside I've installed a second fence which essentially sandwiches the bench top between. This cures the whole movement issue while the jig is in use. I will sometimes throw my surface clamp into one of the holes across the front apron on my bench and clamp things tight. This serves double duty insuring the device is held firm.

The added length of the table section is substantial enough to allow for two fences, front and back. If there ever comes a time when I'm thinking about shooting the edge of some incredibly wide stock and these two fences get in the way then I'll be happy to use an alternate shooting method. For all of my current shooting needs, this size seems generous enough.

Man is a tool-using animal. Nowhere do you find him without tools; without tools he is nothing, with tools he is all.

— Thomas Carlysle

WINDING STICKS

Continuing on with our shop-made arsenal of hand-tool jigs, we'll look at making a reliable set of winding sticks. The winding sticks are nothing more than a pair of straight-grained hardwood batons used to visually exaggerate any warp and twist that can naturally occur in lumber. Before we can try to dimension or flatten any stock for our projects we must first take note of the state of the surfaces waiting to be planed.

Placing the stock on your work bench, lay the winding sticks across the board at each end of the lumber trying best to center each one, as shown at top. Next, stand at one end and eye down the top of the sticks to see how flat the surface is; any small hills or valleys will be amplified through the winding sticks (photo at right). The contrasting strips of hardwood inlaid into the upper edges will help the eye to locate and determine if there is any twist or warp in the wood. Move the winding sticks closer together to narrow

down some smaller locations. Lay them lengthwise, along the work piece, to see if it's straight. Continue this process all over the surface of the board making note of any areas needing attention.

With the aid of the winding sticks we can plainly see which areas need to be addressed. I'll usually scribble some pencil marks in the high spots. After removing the sticks I begin with a jointing plane to flatten the board. This process is detailed in the next chapter, under Preparing Rough Lumber by Hand.

TOP **The winding sticks serve as a visual aid to exaggerate any high or low spots in the surface of our stock.**

ABOVE **Looking across the top of the winding sticks; we can easily see any areas which will need to be worked on. Here you'll notice the far right corner and left nearest side seems to rise up a little ... this is where we'll start planing, re-checking as we go.**

MAKING YOUR OWN STICKS

The time it takes to read this chapter is about all of the time you're going to need to make your own set of winding sticks. Start off with some nice straight-grained stock that's been dried and 'acclimatized' to your own workspace. My sticks are some scraps of straight-grained quarter-sawn mahogany I had left over from a small sail boat I built back in 2005. I milled my lumber down to a finished size of 22"-long by 1⅝"-wide by ½"-thick. At the top of each stick I cut a small ¼"

rabbet to a depth of ³⁄₁₆"-deep. Into this shallow rabbet I laminated a strip of clear maple leaving it a little oversized until the glue set up. Once dry I brought the maple strip down flush to the surface with my block plane and gave everything a light wipe with some polish or wax. Measure and mark a center hole and insert a small nail, dowel or what I used, a small brass rivet. This center mark will serve as a simple referencing aid when laying the sticks down on a work surface to be planed.

The most important area to address when making or working with winding sticks is that they're straight, flat and parallel to one another. I'll regularly check mine for true and with a few light passes with my jointing plane keep them looking and working good. If you ever detect a small warp or hollow in your sticks, try lightly jointing them. If it's any more than ¹⁄₁₆", grab a couple of scraps and make yourself a new set. Flat and straight is the key to accurate results.

½"-thick piece of straight-grained hardwood, with a small rabbet at the top, inlaid with contrasting wood species.

SHOP 'BENTS'

Working in a small woodshop can be a challenge when we're forced to address storage issues, work space, an assembly area, sharpening station ... the list goes on and on. I decided when I moved from my larger shop out East to my small space here in the city that a pair of 'work horses' or 'bents' as I've come to call them would be a welcome addition. Not having the luxury of an assembly area or second bench top surface, they serve as a saw horse from time to time, but mostly address a need for storage space or bench extensions for the components of projects I'm working on here in this small urban space. The first time I noticed this style of work bench/horse came while reading *The Fine Art of Cabinetmaking* by James

RIGHT **A pair of 'bents' can serve many purposes around a small workspace. Actually, they can serve all of these same purposes in a large shop as well! Saw horse, assembly surface, storage shelves, work bench extensions, drying rack…**

Krenov. There was a great shot of his bench room and this form of workshop aid was there next to his bench. I immediately liked the design and decided to build myself a set based on that one image. I'm not exactly sure if he used through tenons or half laps but the design looks pretty close to my eye. When you're ready to build your own set of bents, follow the construction notes here but use these sizes for reference only. I think the real appeal of this design is while building them it's imperative to make their overall dimensions match that of your own workbench. These are the same height as my workbench top and the same overall width of the work surface. This allows them to double as bench top extensions and when moving larger pieces around, from bench top to storage space, it's nice to have somewhere to slide a heavy work piece onto while clearing off an area of the workbench.

I had a few planks of hickory drying in my shop for the better part of three years and decided it would be the perfect species for this project. Because of its strength, straight grain pattern and density, hickory is usually found in items like hammer handles. My bents can pile up with heavy lumber around my shop so the extra strength of hickory is ideal.

As always, begin with straight stock, free of any twist and warp. There's not a whole lot of lumber in these so take the time to find suitable stock. I start off cutting things to length and width. Joint and surface plane everything square before laying out any of the joinery. Carefully measure and mark out the mortises in the feet, legs and top for the stretchers. I'll bore out most of the waste with brace and bit before getting into the chiseling. Once you have the bulk of the waste cleaned out it's time to get out your favorite chisel and grab a mallet. For

To create the mortise shown at left, I first remove the bulk of the waste with brace and bit.

the ends I used a mortising chisel to square up the pocket and a wide bench chisel to clean-up the mortise cheeks. The tenons at the mid point of the legs require a through mortise. To cut these cleanly I'll always put deep scribe lines on the 'show sides' of the legs and starting from the opposite, non-show side, drill down into the cavity about a third

of the way. Next, working with the piece on a bench hook to prevent any damage to my bench, I chisel out the waste, working from the face side to avoid tearing or blowing out the face-side wood fibers. These are only work shop jigs, but it's a good place to practice your hand tool skills! Once all of the mortises are cut and cleaned out, I move on to the tenons.

I like to chop out the mortises first because it's usually an easier task to fit a fat tenon into a mortise then trying to cut out a mortise to match a tenon ... make sense? The

With a mortise chisel, square up the ends of the mortises and chop out the remaining waste.

Clamp and mark out the joinery in both legs simultaneously. This will help to ensure continuity between the pieces.

With a card scraper I'm cleaning up the side of an assembled joint.

tenons should be a nice snug fit, when I do a dry fit I know things are working well when I have to place the dry fit on the floor and while standing on one side, carefully pry out the mating piece. This is what we're looking for, a nice tight fit. Keep the tenons short of the overall depth of the closed mortises; this allows for some play when assembling as well as a place for glue to go.

The through tenons can be cut long and then trimmed flush after final assembly. For a super-strong joint you could easily incorporate a wedged through-tenon here, but

seeing as they're supposed to be a 'quick work-shop aid', I'll do a simple through tenon; a splash of glue and a promise should guarantee they'll last awhile in my workspace. With a hardwood dowel driven through the joints, my grand children will probably be able to swing off of them in forty-five years from now! The top of the legs will be an easy half-lap cut into the stretcher and the leg top. I'll let the top stretchers 'float', meaning no glue or fasteners; it comes in handy sometimes being able to remove the top stretcher when you want to hold an awkward or extremely thick

piece, you simply remove the top stretchers and use the mid-rail as the working surface.

When you're building these for your own work space you may want to think about everything in pairs. By this I mean laying out each mortise, two at a time, cutting out the half-laps with the two legs clamped together assuring they're an exact mate, etc. Cut down the sides of each half-lap joint and remove the bulk waste with a fret saw as you would when cutting through dovetails. After the bulk of the waste has been removed, I used an extremely sharp Japanese style dovetailing chisel to clean things up. Remember that I used hickory to make my set which can rip the edges off a hand tool in a New York minute! Another dry fit and we're almost ready for some glue.

I go over the surface one last time with a cabinet scraper; a great tool for a quick final finish on a piece destined for life in the wood shop.

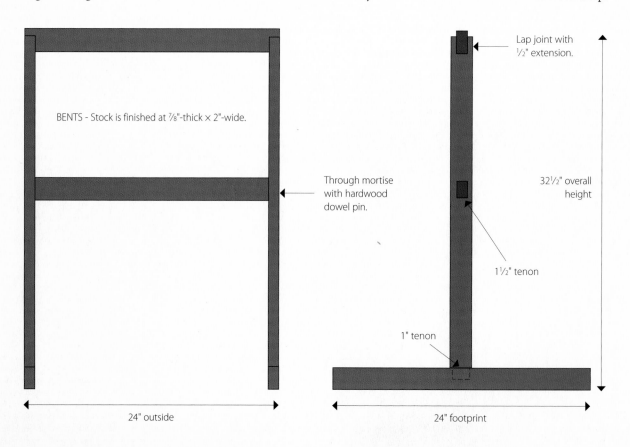

BENTS - Stock is finished at 7/8"-thick × 2"-wide.

Through mortise with hardwood dowel pin.

24" outside

Lap joint with 1/2" extension.

32 1/2" overall height

1 1/2" tenon

1" tenon

24" footprint

A detail that makes a lot of difference during use is cutting a gentle arch on each of the legs, leaving the bents sitting on four corners, rather than two long edges. If your floor is uneven, four corners balance much easier.

The next step is to take the two foot/leg assemblies and attach the mid-stretchers. Some glue and a couple of clamps and we're done. Let this cook for awhile and again, when things are solid I'll drive a couple of dowels through the joint. The top rail can be trimmed to achieve an exact fit and then trim off the dowel stubs still proud of any surfaces. This little project is a great exercise in mortise-and-tenon joinery that will be sure to get you warmed up for the furniture projects in later chapters.

From here it's time for the glue-up. I spread a light amount of glue on the bottom leg tenon cheeks and drive them down into the foot mortises. Clean up any squeeze-out right away so we won't have to worry about it later. Again, this being a shop piece, there's a few liberties we can take with the finish that we wouldn't otherwise have if it was a fine piece of furniture. Let the joint sit for a while allowing the glue to dry and then bore a hole and drive a wooden dowel through the joint. I'll trim all of the dowels flush when the project is completely assembled.

Final glue up; when dry I'll drill and sink a wooden dowel through the joints.

This is a typical day around my shop; the bents are full of the components to some piece being worked on. In this case its parts of the small side table from Chapter 6, 'Skinny Legs and All'.

CHAPTER THREE

Tales, Techniques and Tradition

TAKE A PLANK OF TIMBER AND LOOK AT IT, ROUGH AND ready right out of a saw mill. Twisted and turning, grains roll along as if still being pushed by some outside force. It was in its natural environment not so long ago, still breathing, ever changing. From forest to you, in hand, in shop – your shop or place of work, not too far to fall ... the tree that is.

Beauty hidden under the scars of industry that brought it to this point lying out before you to either embrace it or discard it. Now think about the piece of furniture you'd like to create from it. Imagine in some detail its components, complete. Perhaps an apron on a small side table, tenoned so carefully into its mortises, keeping in mind its final state, finished and flat, welcoming to the touch completely. How do you start with a rough piece of lumber and transform it through these stages of evolution? This is the beginning ... a place where we'll start down through the journey of using hand tools to build furniture.

OPPOSITE **Winters work shop windows.**
February 2007

A PLACE TO BEGIN...

Every project in this book will begin right here, with a cut list and a hand saw, a saw bench and a strong back. Technique and perseverance; an understanding of the time involved, the physical requirements to consider and hopefully the inspiration to continue working in this time-honored way.

If you're in a hurry, then jump past this chapter; keeping in mind that the journey is the destination. You could easily or even, sensibly choose to purchase pre-finished lumber, possibly surface-planed — better yet, surfaced planed and jointed on one side. Maybe it was nicely stacked, measured and hand delivered to your work space or studio. I wonder how many reading this were, or still are, planning to take axe in hand, and march out through the back forty. Reclaimed from the land-fill? Found in front of the neighbors place on 'Yard Waste Removal Day'? (That can be a real good one for you inner-city lumber-jacks!) Whatever method you choose to get your stock on the workbench in front of you is up to you and perfectly fine at both ends of the scale. It's what you'll do with these components after, that really matters.

That said, if you buy (as I sometimes do) reclaimed or rough stock lumber, and want to try dimensioning it by hand, then getting to know and understand the wood you'll be using for a specific task can be no better understood than starting at these milling stages.

To see and to touch, listen and learn from every fiber under your hand, making up all of the components in the projects ahead. You'll notice the changing textures in the reversing grain of that piece of black cherry you were planning on using for the wall cabinet shelf divider. You'll see those tiny hairline cracks creeping out of the end grain in the white oak you wanted to fold into those table tops. All of the smells and sounds of working wood by hand could quickly be lost if you were simply pulling a plank out of the arse-end of a thickness planer. (Not that there's anything wrong with that!)

Standing over a workbench for a morning session of 'scrubbing' can be a rewarding and enlightening experience. Believe me when I say this is not for everyone. Dimensioning rough lumber takes patience and determination. Nothing here is exceptionally difficult, nor will it require a vast number of tools. It will simply be the time that you take in getting to know and truly understand the species of wood you're expecting to work with and create from. Follow the handsaw-to-handplane path, and your chances of up-rooting any hidden surprises from the lumber you've chosen to build with will be greatly increased. Take your time and enjoy the process, admire the swirls and the waves in the wood grain. Like an ocean of ripples, crippled together; twisted in form into one solid state, alive and ever changing, moving and breathing, you can think of it as you're working with the wood. Let's begin.

ASSEMBLING A CUT LIST

When I begin thinking about a new project the first and foremost task is to determine the amount of board feet I'll need. A 'board foot' for those that don't already know is a unit of volume for measuring rough lumber in North America; a 12"-wide by 12"-long by 1"-thick piece of lumber equals one board foot. When we order our lumber this is how the folks down at the mill will measure it; they'll also use a 'quarter' system for board thickness as well so it's a good idea to be aware of it. A piece of wood that's one inch thick is referred to as 4/4 (four quarter) then up to 5/4 which translates to $1\frac{1}{4}$". 8/4 is a piece 2 inches thick and so on ... makes sense? Good. This will get your 'wood lingo' going before you're on the phone trying to translate the jargon the mill guy is spitting out at you.

So now that we speak the language of wood we can think about getting a cut list together. My process is first studying the piece and writing down in point form all of the components the finished piece will be made of. I figure out as I go all of the lengths, widths and thicknesses and include my joinery into these numbers. Take your time and try not to overlook those little hidden members inside of a piece: the drawer guides and runners, the sub assembly of the bottom frame, door and drawer pulls, etc.

If working off of a plan or a project from a book (like this one) I'll read through the entire project chapter on the specific piece and make a rough sketch of the design. This again helps me establish my cut list and gets all of the components clear in my head. You don't need a drafting table or need to have artistic skills to accomplish this; just gather the information and make sure you understand what each piece is doing in relation to the next. If you're working off of an existing design then you have the benefit of studying an actual piece in the flesh (so to speak) but one disadvantage is you generally can't see the joinery. This leads to some educated guess work and speculation. You'll have the liberties of using your own favorite joinery techniques but I'd recommend hitting the books to try to find written examples of similar type pieces to have a point of reference when making crucial decisions on joinery applications.

As you work your way down through a list, take into account

CUT LIST - SKINNY LEGS...

FRAME
- 4 LEGS - 1¼" SQUARE x 29⅝" LONG
- 2 APRONS - 16¼" WIDE x 1¹³⁄₁₆" HIGH x ¾" THICK
- 2 RAILS - 10⅞" LONG x 1¹⁄₁₆" HIGH x ⅝" THICK
- 2 TOP SUPPORTS - 11½" LONG x 1³⁄₁₆" WIDE x ½" THICK
- 1 DIVIDER - 12⅜" LONG x 1" WIDE x ½" THICK

BOTH?
- 1 UPRIGHT - 4⅛" LONG x 1⁵⁄₁₆" WIDE x ⁹⁄₁₆" THICK

DRAWER BOX
- 2 TOP/BOTTOM BOX - 12¹⁵⁄₁₆" WIDE x 11⅜" DEEP x ⁷⁄₁₆" THICK
- 2 SIDES - 10¹³⁄₁₆" LONG x 7½" HIGH x ⁷⁄₁₆" THICK
- 1 DIVIDER - 10⅛" LONG x 1⅞" WIDE x ⁹⁄₁₆" THICK
- 4 GUIDES - 9¹¹⁄₁₆" LONG x ½" HIGH x ⅜" THICK   *OFFCUT. NOT CRITICAL - USE WHAT YOU HAVE!
- 2 RUNNERS - 9¹¹⁄₁₆" LONG x 1³⁄₁₆" WIDE x ½" THICK

TABLE TOP - 1 TOP - 20" WIDE x 14" DEEP x 1¹⁄₁₆" THICK

BACK PANEL - 11⁵⁄₁₆" W. x 7⅞" H. x ⁵⁄₃₂" THICK.

DRAWERS
- 1 FRONT -
- 2 FRONTS -   FIGURE AFTER FRAME COMPLETE!
- 2 SIDES -
- 4 SIDES -

'board foot calculators' available online; most are simple to use and will generate a total board foot count for you. You punch in the length, width and thickness of each piece and work down through your list. Hit the total at the end and you're in business. That said, I often have a hard time trusting anything I see or read on the internet so I've learned how to do this myself for good measure; at least I'll be able to get a second opinion. Try it out and see for yourself.

WOOD SELECTION

I think it would be foolish of me to try to tell you what to look for when choosing the stock for the projects ahead. There have been so many books already written on the subject of wood and wood species, properties and uses. I do hope that if you've already committed to this stage of the process, where you'd like to build furniture using only hand tools, then you've already done some homework on the medium we'll be working with.

With a cut list in hand, or at least hanging on the wall in plain view for all to see, select the appropriate stock for the project. When satisfied with the look of the piece, again checking for twists, cracks and checks or any other undesirable characteristics, measure and mark with a square, being sure to allow for some love. I usually add a good ½" to each end, an inch over-all, for squaring later on. Now that we have our stock rough cut to length we'll take it to our work bench to establish one flat face.

the board widths in particular. If a cabinet side is finished at 16"-wide then it's safe to assume you won't be using one wide piece of wood to make it. You'll probably be edge jointing up some narrower material to make up this width. Have a look around and see what your area offers in common board widths. The mill I use sometimes has some nice wide boards in the 9" to 10" or even 12" range but generally the 6" to 8" range is a good bet. Get to know the people you're getting your lumber from so you'll be aware of their common sizes and watch for any of those special times when they do get in wider than usual stock.

The formula to calculate board feet, as mentioned, is (in inches)

length × width × thickness, then divide that number by 144. Once you have the entire list assembled, simply follow this formula and add up the sums. Another general rule of thumb seems to be to add anywhere from 20% to 35% extra for waste when calculating your cut list order. Again get to know the wood and your mill so you'll be able to make a better judgment when adding extra on for any checks, cracks, splits or other undesirable characteristics. My mill seems to have really nice, clear stock so when I order my lumber my waste factor can be minimal. If I have extra at the end of a project, all the better!

For those of you that use the internet, there are quite a few free

PREPARING LUMBER- SCRUB

A quick look over each face will determine where to start. Pick the side that looks the best; really, it's that simple. Holding the work down between some bench dogs, use your winding sticks, laying each stick across the width at each end of the plank. Look down and along the board, then move the sticks and check again across the width of the stock. If the piece to be worked is large then I recommend you mark any 'sculpted' areas with either chalk or a dark pencil. Any valleys or hills should be carefully noted. This will help to identify any problems in the piece as we progress towards flatter planes ahead. On smaller boards you can probably just trust your eyes and your hands.

With a scrub plane set to take an aggressive cut, (between $^1/_{16}$" - $^1/_8$"), work the surface diagonally down the stock, overlapping each pass with the previous until you've reached the opposite corner. Follow with a second pass cutting in the opposite diagonal direction. This 'cross-grain' cutting action is what some people refer to as 'a controlled tear'. Cutting almost across the grain to remove waste and getting closer to flatness. Check your work often as you go. Try to be honest with the stock and with yourself. If you only go halfway at this stage, and you tell yourself that it's good enough and it isn't, then you'll only be defeating any chances of success later on as the project progresses. Take your time and make it FLAT!

When you think you've got it somewhat close, take a full sweep traveling with the grain over the entire surface.

To determine grain direction I always remembered this saying.

"Pith side, plane with the Points."

The 'Pith side' is the inside of the tree which can easily be determined by looking at the direction of the rings on the stock ends; and the 'Points' are those cathedral shapes in the grain. This works for me 99% of the time when I have to determine which way I should be planing.

Loosen the dogs and flip the piece over. Place your fingers on opposite corners and try rocking it. Look for any movement and try to determine and locate any hills still creating this see-sawing effect. Hit these areas again with the scrub plane, being careful now to take lighter passes. Again, turn the stock over to check for flatness. Keep repeating these steps until the first face is flat. Using a fine marking gauge, scribe a line around the edges of the board making sure to reference off of the flat face. This will be the final thickness of the board so we'll want this line to be nice and deep, accurate and true.

Turn the piece over and clamp it down again in the bench dogs. We'll follow the same steps on this side until we've reached a desirable flatness with the scrub plane. This time though we'll go further in the finishing process, moving to our jointing plane and checking our reference line often, making sure we don't over-shoot the finished thickness we're after. I'll do a complete surface pass starting at the nearest edge, working across and along the entire surface of the board. Check your progress again using the winding sticks. Take notice if one corner is higher than the other. When the corners of the winding sticks line up perfectly over the boards length, we're done. Turn the board back over to the first face we flattened with the scrub plane and joint it.

You can put away the jointing plane and grab your favorite smoothing plane at this point; however, when I'm milling a lot of stock in one session I'll sometimes keep scrubbing and jointing all of the stock needed for the entire project. Then when complete I'll smooth the entire lot at once. It's perfectly fine to bring each board to a finished state, one at a time, through each stage of operation. The choice is yours, whatever feels comfortable for you. Working at a pace that makes sense to your mind and body is extremely important to achieving success when working wood. Have a glass of water; take a walk around the bench a few times, whatever you need.

EDGE JOINTING

With two surfaces flat we can clamp the piece and joint its edge again either using the jointing plane or for smaller-scale work a jack plane; check often to see that you're planning square to the face. When one edge is square we'll scribe the overall width of the piece, a nice deep cut for the saw to follow is best. Grab your favorite rip saw and go at it on the saw bench. Rip the piece

staying just outside of the scribe line; we'll get it right to size with the jointing plane next.

Clamp it up again on edge and finish this second edge off with the jointer.

SHOOT

With four sides flat and square it's time to address the ends of the stock. I like to shoot one end on my shooting board. Now with five sides good to go, we'll measure and mark the last end and on the saw bench, cross-cut it making sure to leave the scribe line. Put the stock back on the shooting board and bring the piece to our perfectly finished length.

Six-faces, all square, flattened and finished by hand; take a deep breath and admire your work for a moment or two; for this is only the beginning...

SAWING BY HAND

When we enter the realm of building furniture using only hand tools, our approach to projects and the steps we take to working on a piece must inevitably change. This is nowhere more obvious than when we dimension our rough stock using hand saws. In a power tool shop we can rip and then cross cut all of the components to a certain project at the Table saw in a relatively short time span while not ever breaking a sweat. I'm not sure that the same could be said in the hand tool workshop. Ripping operations may be broken into sub-categories as they may become quite overwhelming and tedious. Perhaps a more reasonable way of dimensioning our lumber is to take certain structural components' of the project and take them through each step of finishing.

IE: Cross-cutting and then ripping all of the pieces for say the

Cross cutting some cherry for the post and panel cabinet.

drawers in a certain project. Get all of the different pieces to a certain achievable place and then backtrack and bring another 'set' of components to the same place. This will indeed break up the repetition of ripping all of the pieces of a project at once; not to mention saving your arm muscles from certain doom! When sawing by hand, although is not incredibly strenuous, the techniques used must be observed, practiced and then executed to achieve favorable results. Watch what you do and take note of any errors that may re-occur while you work. For a long time I noticed that when performing any rip cuts I'd tend to lean over

to one side and end up with an out of square edge. This was never really that big of a deal since the angle would always seem to fall away from my scribe line. A little more 'fat' to cut off later so no worries. If however my cuts were seemingly always drifting into and then over my cut line, then practicing while holding a square to the edge of your saw plate will help develop a feel of ripping square stock.

CROSS CUTTING

Take the stock to be sawn and place it along either your saw bench or a saw hook at your bench top, measure it and mark it using a square.

And you thought I had a hand plane problem…

Some people like using pencils, others a marking knife; I use both on some really dark woods but usually a pencil for most. When you first start using a hand saw I recommend marking the cut line across the boards face and also down the opposite edge. Place the heel of your cross cut saw on the outside half of the line, making sure to keep the other half of the line between you and your saw. This will ensure you can always see your path to cut to. With your free hand, lightly press your thumb on the saw blade to keep it grounded and 'complete the circle' so to speak. Start to establish a light kerf by pulling the saw back towards you a few times at an angle in the neighborhood of 25°. Once you have the kerf established you can then lightly push down to start your cut. Try to use as much of the blade as possible and eye down over the far edge of the stock to follow the square edge, keep a solid yet light grasp on the saw handle, work your way across the face trying to maintain a 45° angle. Take your time and enjoy the process making sure when you approach the end of the cut your stock is well supported to avoid any bottom tear out from the piece.

RIPPING

To start the Rip cut you can follow the same procedures as you did when cross-cutting. Establishing a saw kerf, start down the line, again keeping half of the cut line between you and your saw plate. The main difference of the rip cut is the saw should be kept at a higher angle relative to the stock, somewhere in the 60° range is desirable. Try to use the full length of the blade, taking your time and letting the saw do the work. When ripping smaller scale stock I'll often use my tail vise and from a more 'upright' position can move pretty quickly down the length of the board.

THE DOVE'S TALE

dove·tail
Pronunciation [duhv-teyl]
 – noun.
1. a Tenon broader at its end than at its base; pin.
2. a joint formed of one or more such tenons fitting tightly within corresponding mortises.

Pertaining To Drawers
It's an all too familiar story to open a book, magazine or web page and discover another word on dovetails. From lay-out to execution, styles and errors, everyone has an opinion. That in itself is reason to write about the topic to some degree.

A universal signature placed to display? Or, simply the strongest joint for the needed application?

Consider a drawer side, solid wood usually in the $3/8$" to $1/2$" thickness, always moving, pushing and pulling; nails and glue? Dowels and rabbets?

All methods have proven the tests of time through woodworkers of the past. Thousands of years displayed in every one, some for the better and some ... not. With that, let's talk dovetails.

To show the processes of both a through dovetail as well as a half

Dovetailed drawers and box.

blind, let's stroll through the stages of constructing a traditional drawer.

Half blind dovetails at the front, with through dovetails in the back. This will follow the lay-out through to sawing and get you better acquainted with the procedure. The principals of cutting a dovetail in a drawer side are basically the same as cutting dovetails in a side cabinet 8' long. Once you lay things out it really doesn't matter how many or how few you plan to do.

Stock Preparation

Success in any style of furniture building always starts at the same place, proper stock selection and preparation. You can't expect to achieve satisfactory results in a finished piece if you start with poorly prepared lumber. Once you have everything dimensioned, a quick going over with the smoothing plane and we're ready. The closer the components are to a finished state the better. As for fitting the drawer pieces here's a tip: Make the front and the back pieces a shade bigger than the drawer opening, so you can just squeeze them into their openings. You'll plane them to an exact fit later. As for the sides, they should be an exact fit in height and the lengths should be about $3/8$" shorter than the depth of the drawer opening to allow for any movement later on.

The Layout

Before I get into the actual lay-out of the pieces I like to gather up all of the tools I'm going to need to complete the process. In this case I'll be using a marking gauge, a marking knife, a dovetail marker, a plough plane, a skew angle block plane, two sets of dividers, assorted dovetail chisels, a mallet and finally and perhaps foremost my 15 tpi, (teeth per inch) dovetail saw. Make sure your tools are well sharpened before you begin.

The tools used in making a dovetailed drawer.

The first step before you do anything else is to determine where the drawer bottom will be located in the finished drawer. Marking in a line with a pencil or marking knife isn't enough; what I do to eliminate any chance of error is to take my plough plane and actually cut the drawer bottom groove. I like to place my drawer bottom about a $1/4$" up from the bottom of the drawer sides and make a $3/16$" groove. For larger drawers the bottom width could be increased as well as the spacing under the panel.

The next step is to transfer all of the drawer pieces thicknesses to their mating pieces; i.e. the drawer side's thickness will be scribed on the drawer front inside and the drawer back pieces; the drawer front thickness will be scribed on the sides etc. With a marking gauge, cut a clean, deep line to register your saw and chisels to.

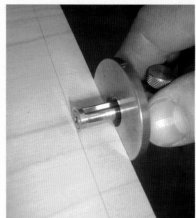

LEFT **My small plough plane makes quick work of locating the dado for the drawers bottom panel.**

BELOW **Scribing components thicknesses with marking gauge.**

The "140 Trick"

I first saw Rob Cosman do this and he had mentioned seeing Alan Peters using this method; I wonder where Alan saw it? No matter...

The step is called the '140 Trick' because a skewed angle block plane, the original being the Stanley #140, is used. Set the fence on the plane so you'll be taking a shallow cut the width of the scribe line you made in the previous step. One or two light passes on the inside edges of the drawer sides is all that's needed to create a small shoulder. This shallow rabbet will make life a lot easier when we have to transfer our tails over to our pin boards later on. The usual way to carry out this step is to hold the cut-out dovetail pin board over the mating piece and using your eye, you transfer your lines over with a scribe knife. This leaves room for error so by doing the 140 trick; the small shoulder eliminates the guess work and insures an accurate transfer of lines. Now that we have our drawer bottom groove cut as well as our shoulders we can go ahead and lay-out the actual dovetails.

Cutting a very shallow rabbet with my Skew angle block plane.

Mark off the two outside shoulders. We'll use it to match the other side of the piece.

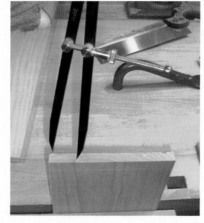

Walking out the spacing…

'Over-stepping' determines eventual pin size.

Marking out the tails

To do this we use two sets of dividers. One will be set to the desired thickness of each outside pin and the other will come to represent one tail plus one pin's width.

Start with defining the width at each outside edge of the drawer. I usually make this somewhere between $3/16"$ and $1/4"$. Create a small indent in the stock on each side and lay this first set of dividers aside. We'll be using that same measurement later on.

Take your other set of dividers and starting at the indent you just made at one edge, walk them across until you reach the opposite side. You should try to finish just a little past the opposite indentation you marked in the last step. This small space between your first indent and the final walking mark will come to represent the width of each pin.

A dovetail marker makes drawing the square line and the slope line trouble-free.

If you finish with too much space, close-up your dividers a little. If when you walk across and find you pass over the opposite side, then open them up a bit.

A bit of trial and error will get you to the desired width you're after. Just remember not to press down too hard so you don't make any indents until you have the proper spacing's set. Once you achieve your desired widths go ahead and walk back across, this time leaving marks as you go.

When you reach the other side, lift the dividers and starting from the first indent you made, walk back across in the opposite direction. This will leave a series of marks across the end of your stock representing your tails and pins. Now that you have the top distances stepped out with tiny dimples to capture your pencil or knife edge, we'll look at dovetail angles. There has been much stated and debated on the sloping angle in dovetailing. A general rule is in the 1:6 to 1:8 ratio. These numbers basically mean that for every inch traveled across a base line, there is a 6 to 8 inch rise (see diagram). I think aesthetics play a big role in deciding what angle to use, I find if I'm doing one large dovetail in a structural application, i.e. a side tables top rail mating into the top of a leg, I'll use a lesser

angle thus, creating a wider tail. For slighter drawer sides, I'll go with a 1:8 ratio. Cleaner, almost quieter they're just as structurally sound; try them all on some scrap wood until you develop your own opinions. Trust your eyes.

When you mark in your cut lines be careful not to draw down past the scribe marks. This will help train your eye when cutting out your tails and not cutting down past the shoulders. Also remember to take your pencil and 'scribble' in the waste area; you'd be surprised at how easy it is to mistakenly cut out an area you're not supposed to.

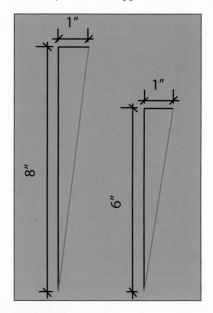

1:8 and 1:6 dovetail ratios.

Lie Nielson 15 tpi dovetail saw; setting a standard in today's work shop.

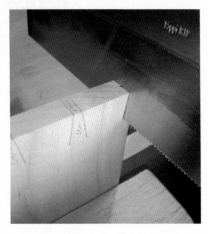

Leaving half of the line…

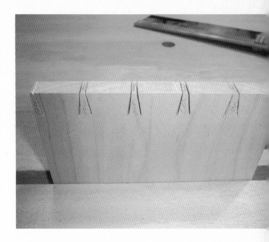

Tails straight and square.

From here it's time to finally reach for the dovetail saw and make some sawdust.

Sawing the Dovetails

Now that we've laid out our dovetails it's time to reach for the saw and cut them out. I use a western style dovetail saw, however there seems to be an equal amount of wood workers using a Japanese style pull saw. I've tried both and own both. The Japanese variety can do amazing things in delicate, tight places however, I usually reach for the western style in most of my scale work. I encourage you to try both, develop a feel and a taste and you'll soon find out quite easily for yourself which one suits you and your own style.

When cutting out the tails it's important to cut as close to the line as possible without cutting away all of it. If you cut all of your line away you'll have no reference mark. That said, you want to try to actually 'split' the line; this will eliminate the amount you'll need to pare away later on.

When I cut dovetails I usually start on the right hand side of my piece (being right-handed I suppose) and then cut every other cheek. This is so I'm not going back and forth from one angle to another. I do all of one and then the other. And remember, always be aware of the shoulder lines, try to never cut past these as it will really stand out in the finished piece.

Also make sure to make the top of your cuts square to the piece. If you go off of your line on the way down the slope it's not really a big deal at this point. You still have to transfer these cuts over to the pin board so if the angle is slightly off it won't affect the final piece. However, if you don't make the end grain cut of the board square, your pieces will never line up properly in assembly.

Removing the Waste

At this stage most people grab a chisel and start chopping out the waste. This is a very time consuming and can be rather risky. I prefer to first take a fret saw with a blade that has a narrower kerf than the dovetail saw I used and cut out the bulk of the waste. Simply bring the fret saw blade down the kerf to the bottom, give it a slight twist and start your cut. Try to stay at least 1/8" above the scribe line to be safe. After you get all of the waste cut out between the tails, we can get set to chop out the remaining area using a mallet and chisel.

I use a mallet when chopping out the waste for better control. Always start your cut from the inside, non showing face of the piece being careful not to cut all the way through.

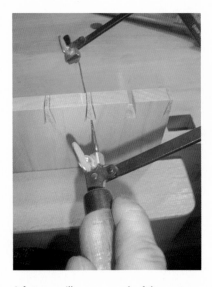

A fret saw will remove much of the waste. Keep a keen eye on the base line; you don't want to saw down past it!

The vertical cut down the inside shoulder.

Cleaning up the shoulder with a delicate detail chisel.

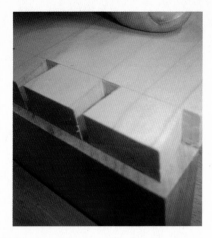

The 140 Trick shows what it's made of…

Sighting down, following through; this is something to practice.

Then, turn the piece over so the outside, face side is up and finish the cut. This ensures that if you blow out some of the wood it won't be on the show side of the dovetail.

Finish off by mounting the piece vertically in a vise and cleaning out the inside corners. I use my detail chisels which are perfect for this job. They are designed to be used with hand force only so you have optimum control over the cut.

TRANSFER TO THE PIN BOARD

Now that we have the tails all cut out we can transfer these over to our pin boards. I mount the un-marked pin board, along with a block of wood, in my shoulder vise and create a flush surface to register the 140 Trick shoulder cut we made earlier on. This small shoulder enables us to line these two pieces up without any trouble whatsoever.

This always seems to be the point where any mistakes occur in the dovetail process. Anyone can practice cutting to a line and chopping out waste with a chisel, but if you can't transfer the tails over to the pin board with dead-on accuracy, then you'll never have a perfect fitting joint.

Now that you have the tail board straddled across the end of the pin board, take a sharp knife and scribe the cheeks of the tails. I make a

series of light cuts making sure to keep my knife blade tight against the cheeks of the dovetails. When you have your knife marks laid out along side of the tails, take the pin board and set it up in your shoulder vice vertically, facing away from you.

Again with your dovetail marker, finish marking off the vertical lines down the inside face with a very sharp pencil being sure not to draw down past the scribe lines.

CUTTING AND CHOPPING THE PINS

Now that all of the pins have been properly laid out, take your dovetail saw and cut down each cheek again being careful not to pass through the lower scribe lines. This cut can be a challenge since you have to cut on a 45 degree angle and follow two lines at once. You only need to cut to the lines; the rest of the material will be removed with a chisel.

Once the cheek of each pin is cut down with the dovetail saw, it's time to chop out the waste. Again I use my Japanese dovetail chisels for this job. Try to take shallow cuts and stay clear of the bottom of the socket. Once we chop out the waste with our piece lying flat on the bench top, we'll put it in our shoulder vise and work on a vertical axis to complete the pins. I like to put a scrap

board on the bench when chopping out the pins to protect the bench top from any stray chisel cuts. Use a mallet and take shallow cuts.

When chopping out waste there's a few points to think about. Firstly, try to use the widest chisel possible for each cut. This means if you have a one inch area to cut, use a one inch chisel to do it. This is most important when making the final cut on the scribe line. Another point is after you make a few vertical cuts down, take a moment and clear out the waste with a horizontal, paring style cut. This helps keep the socket area clear of debris and prevent a blow-out in the pin board. Every step at this point is crucial; if you mess up now, you'll have a long way to go back to fix it. One of the nice things in custom cabinet making is continuity. Each drawer face is chosen for its grain pattern and drawers that may run side-by-side, one area to the next all getting cut from a single board. That way the grain pattern can run across an entire cabinet or flow gracefully up the face of a cabinet. This would be a bad spot to mess up a dovetail pin and have to make a new drawer front; you'd lose that 'flow' and could upset the balance of the overall design.

Now that the waste is cut out to each scribe line, it's time to put the

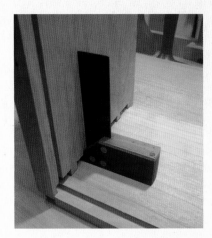

Chop out the waste in the half blind dovetails.

Sockets clean and ready for the next step.

Checking a dry fit.

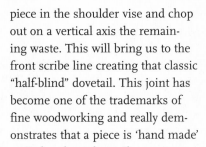

piece in the shoulder vise and chop out on a vertical axis the remaining waste. This will bring us to the front scribe line creating that classic "half-blind" dovetail. This joint has become one of the trademarks of fine woodworking and really demonstrates that a piece is 'hand made'

In hand cut dovetails, you can make the pins as thin as the kerf of your saw will allow. Visually I like a pin that finishes off a little bit less than ¼". This gives the drawer a kind of finesse look as well as keeping the structural integrity of the joint intact. When the drawer side is put into the vise it's also a good idea to sandwich a backer board in as well. This will help prevent any blow-out during the chopping process. When the scribe lines are reached, I take my detail chisels and clean-up the entire inside corners and faces. Keeping the lot square and smooth, try not the damage the corners and edges, a gentle touch and proper care will make assembly a lot less painful. Work neatly!

When everything is cut out we can do a dry fit. Using hand pressure only, tap the pieces together to see how things are going to line up. Have a close look at each surface and if things look a little too tight, mark it with a pencil and pare a little bit away being careful to take

very shallow cuts. It's a whole lot easier to cut off more than it is to add wood back on to a piece. Check for square as well, checking your diagonals as you go. Another small tip, make sure to bevel the inside edges of the tails at this point as well. It's easier to do this now, while the drawer is disassembled. When it's time to glue things up I like to start off again with laying out everything I'll need i.e. hammer, glue, rags, clamps, small spatula or stick for spreading the glue. Take your time and make sure things are

remaining square as you go. Once complete put the drawer aside and fit the drawer bottom.

Crafting a traditional style drawer like this is a challenge that will prove to be very enjoyable. It takes more time than simpler design variations (about a full day in the shop) but the results are well worth the extra work. A well-fitted drawer will last for generations and every time someone opens it, those half-blind dovetails will stand-out and proudly show the hand-made quality that went into making them.

Ready for glue.

mor•tise
Pronunciation [mawr-tis] –noun
1. a notch, hole, groove, or slot made in a piece of wood or the like to receive a tenon of the same dimensions.

ten•on
Pronunciation [ten-uhn] –noun
1. a projection formed on the end of a timber or the like for insertion into a mortise of the same dimensions.

THE MORTISE AND THE TENON

The timber frame, so structurally sound like the institution of family, always impartial to the traditions of time. We're reminded of these thoughts and witness through our minds eye something to behold in wood ... fixed mechanically

timbers leaning

never falling

until pushed

by some outside force.

through joinery, chopped by hand in an earlier place. Another time when our ancestors spoke of legend, abandoned for generations some arrangement, or scheme, perhaps even a system to learn. A great Schooner ship's rib structure, internally skeletal, ripped up onto a shoreline like a great whale beached and stranded for all to glimpse lying across the strand. These images are perfect exhibits of the true power of wooden joinery. Sitting quietly, some are the better part of 5,000 years old, 'wooden bones' lying dormant all over the world. A pinnacle ever so brief in the eyes of history ... From an old cattle barn still standing after 150 years, down in the valley, never disturbed, to massive

ABOVE LEFT **Timber Frame next to my shop. Stacked and waiting – patiently. Autumn 2007.**

ABOVE RIGHT **Components of a trestle table. Two precious planks I purchased from a friend's boat shop in Nova Scotia. Reclaimed from a barge in Martha's Vineyard where they lay for the better part of 100 years.**

hand hewn timbers in the heart of every metropolis, the trendy studio lofts with uncovered beams, exasperatingly expensive with the stylish markets gushing with passer-buyers always rushing, moving just out of reach of these monuments of man.

Mrs. Mortise, meet Mr. Tenon.

So simply coupled, collectively bonded, perfectly together.

THE MORTISE

Without sounding too redundant, start with straight, squared stock. The layout of a mortise and tenon is something open to interpretation however; the method I find best suited for the work I do and the tools I use is as follows.

A rule of thirds is something I follow whenever I can. It is the process of determining the overall width of the stock being mortised and/or tenoned and then dividing that width by three. Three-quarter inch material as an example would have a quarter-inch sidewall, a quarter-inch mortise/tenon and finally another quarter-inch wall or cheek.

I try to follow this generalized rule for most mortise and tenon applications. One deviation that comes to mind is when a design calls for an offset apron or perhaps a different design element where you don't want the pieces joined to finish flush.

There are as many construction methods for cutting mortise and tenons as there are mortise and tenon variations. Almost every example shares this commonality: the tenon cheek-to-mortise side is crucial for proper glue-ups and over all strength. We'll look at a couple of examples used in the projects outlined in this book beginning with a closed mortise and then on to a 'bridal slip' I like to use for frame and panel style doors. Proper layout is an essential step that needs to be slowly and accurately executed.

Let's start off with that.

Beginning with brace and bit, I will remove the bulk of the waste in the mortise. I use a small piece of painter's tape wrapped around the end of the bit to give myself a pre-determined depth in the mortise.

Examples of marking gauges, a single cutter, a dedicated mortising blade and a traditional pin style gauge.

My marking gauge has a mortising attachment, which allows me to
mark both sides, and walls of the
cavity simultaneously, but I should
confess I rarely use it. I establish the
location of the mortise and with a
square, then use a pencil to draw in
my mortise's top and bottom. I also
like to mark off the shoulders of the
tenon just for a point of reference.
I will then use my single-bladed
marking gauge to scribe deep cuts
down each cheek.

I find it just as efficient to scribe
the one side and then the other
using a single blade-marking gauge.
If you do use a single-bladed marking gauge, be sure to reference it
off of the same side of the work
piece. The older pin style marking
gauges can also work well but only
when properly dressed and filed.
Otherwise they tend to tear out the
fibers rather than cut them.

Once both sides of the mortise
are cleanly scored. The top and bottom scribe lines need to be marked
with a marking knife and square. I
have seen some examples of people
scribing all of the way across the
face of the mortised piece however,
this only leads to extra planing and
a chance for added error later on.
Another option is only to scribe
one side of the mortise allowing
your chisel to determine the width.
This can work but taking an extra
few seconds and scribing the entire
perimeter of the cavity improves the
odds at successful joinery. When
choosing mortise and tenoning
tools it's also a good idea to use a
common width throughout your
tool selections.

What I mean is if you tend to
work in three-quarter inch stock,
then use a one-quarter inch tool;
auger bit, chisel, plane iron, etc ...
it allows for easier set-up and pre-
determines things for you. No need
to chop one side of the mortise and
then move on to the other with thin-

Scribing the sides of the mortise.

Setting pin style gauge directly off of chisel width.

Removing the remaining waste and chopping to the line with a dedicated mortise chisel.

Chopping a mortise with dedicated chisel and heavy, shop made mallet.

Top: $1/4$" Henry Taylor Swan Neck
Bottom: $1/4$" Lie-Nielson Mortising Chisel

ner bladed tools. We can easily find top quality products form reliable dealers offering well made mortising tools in a variety of widths.

Larger applications demand larger-scale tools so one may consider turning to a heavier, timber framing style product. Massive irons and heavy 'Commander' type mallets can chop away the hardest woods. With that said, how much chopping, hammering and well, sweating is necessary? My preference is to remove the bulk of the waste with a brace and bit. A pleasure to use, quality reclaimed braces are readily available at flea markets and in most antique tool shops. Bits can be a little more difficult to find but there are a couple of manufacturers still available. (Refer to Reference sec-

tion) If you follow this method and use a drill or brace to remove the waste, it's a good idea to mark a center line when laying out the joint. Begin with locating the top and bottom of the mortise and follow with a center line. Then, following the methods described above, continue and mark out the sidewalls. This center line will provide an accurate location for the drill or auger bit.

Once you've removed the bulk of the waste, take your mortising chisel and carefully finish removing the material. I'll start just shy off the bottom scribe line and clear away the remaining, internal material. Then, setting the chisel directly in the scribe line, chop down to the finished depth. A simple wood block can help to keep things

square. I will sometimes use a specialty chisel for cleaning out deeper mortises which can tend to be a little tricky with a common-style mortise chisel. A swan neck style chisel is the ideal tool for this and can be purchased at most specialty tool dealers. Keep in mind that the bottom of the mortise should be a little deeper than the over-all length of the tenon, say $1/16$" greater than the desired depth. Another point to mention is the bottom of the mortise, don't worry too much on the state of it, no one will ever see it so it doesn't have to be smooth.

When you have your mortise complete, take a few light shavings with a smoothing plane to remove your scribe lines and clean up the face. Now you can prepare the tenon.

THE TENON

Again, starting with freshly planed, square stock, mark off the shoulders of the tenon using your marking gauge of choice. From here we can establish the width and length either with a ruler and by measuring the mortise opening, or by laying the tenon stock over the mortise and actually scribing the thicknesses. This eliminates any errors that can occur during measuring. I'm actually one who uses a measuring tape or ruler only when I absolutely need to. If I can, I always prefer scribing a piece laid off of its mate, or perhaps when determining the length of a component, then again I'll lay the piece into its desired finished place and scribe its finished length instead of measuring it.

Once we have the tenon scribed it's time to chuck the piece into your vise and make some saw dust. I start off with the long cheek cuts of the tenon followed by the cross cut determining the tenon's length. Something to consider when laying out your joinery is the depth of the tenons cheeks. If you're building a substantial piece which could easily have a tenon in the 2$\frac{1}{2}$"-deep neighborhood, does your saw have enough depth in it's plate to cut them out?

Since you'll be ripping the wood, (cutting down through the end grain), you'll have to use a rip saw.

For shallow tenons I'll grab my dovetail saw and proceed as normal however, when I'm dealing with larger joints, the brass back of the backsaw will bottom out at the top of the kerf preventing me from completing my cut. This can be one of those occasions where it's nice to have the luxury of simply reaching for your larger, rip style carcass or full-size tenon saw. Having the extra blade depth is really handy in larger joinery applications.

One alternative is to purchase a reasonably priced Japanese style

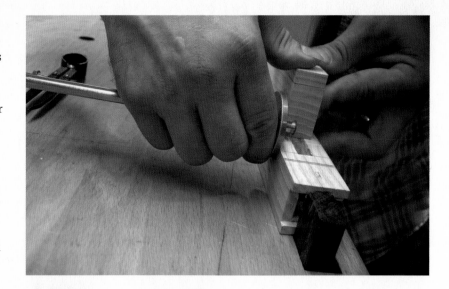

ABOVE Scribe the tenons thickness directly off of the mortise. A kind of 'in-line story stick'? This is far more accurate than measuring. Dividers may also be a reliable way to safely and accurately transfer measurements.

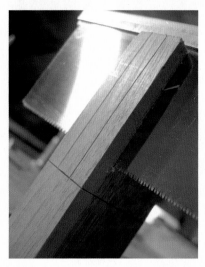

LEFT This shallow saw blade is unable to finish the depth of cut in this tenon example. The brass back of the saw prematurely bottoms out.

Ryoba saw. These saws have no backs and have both cross-cut and rip pattern teeth. This can be used to complete the cut if your smaller rip saw bottoms out before you reach your desired depth.

Some woodworkers like to set the stock to be cut on an angle to make these long cuts, trying to follow both lines at once; I prefer to keep the work piece straight, or better said, level in my shoulder vise and beginning at the furthest side away from me, establish a straight kerf along the end grain. Then, once I have a nice, straight saw kerf to guide my blade, I'll begin the vertical plunge down through the wood fibers. Slowly follow your scribe line being sure not to cut beyond the bottom

shoulder. Once finished, repeat the process for the other side.

Something to consider when making this second cut is this: do you leave the work piece in the vise as is; simply stepping or moving the saw over to the second scribe line? Or, do you rotate the workpiece in the vise so you're essentially making the exact same cut as before, (at least in set-up form anyway). Stop and think about it for a second when you begin that initial cut. Is it more comfortable to start sawing the scribe line closer or further away from your body? Either way you have to be sure to keep the saw blade on the 'waste side' of the scribe line. Better yet, keeping the saw blade perfectly splitting the scribe line to the waste side!

When all of the vertical cuts are complete, reposition the work piece in your vise or on your miter hook and make the cross-cuts. I like to stay just inside my scribe lines and then pair away the remaining waste with a chisel or small shoulder plane. Once complete, test fit your tenon. It should be a nice tight fit but not too tight that you have to use a hammer to fit them together. Reasonable hand force should be all that's necessary. If it's still too tight, take shallow passes with a finely-set shoulder plane taking a pass from one side and then the other. This will ensure the tenon remains in the position you wanted and doesn't become lopsided from one shoulder to the next. Again a test fit and we're there.

If you test fit the tenon and it's too loose, you need to decide how loose? When you insert the tenon into the mortise you should be able to comfortably and confidently hold the mortise piece upright with the tenoned piece standing out at a perfect ninety-degree angle and not fall out. If your wiggle test determines that it is indeed a loose fitting joint, simply take a scrap from your off cut pile and cut out a thin shim which can be glued onto the cheek that's over-cut. When dry you should be able to correct the error again with shallow passes from a shoulder plane or rabbeting block plane. When we're happy with the fit I like to plane a small chamfer into the

tenoned edges, this will make things run a little smoother when it comes time for assembly and also gives somewhere for the glue to go.

Another procedure I will often do to up the ante in the strength-factor of a joint would be to add a dowel through the center of the mortise once it's assembled.

Another alternative you could consider is drawboring things for a really tight seam. The process of drawboring is relatively simple and not too dissimilar than a standard doweled joint. Here's a quick explanation of the drawbored mortise-and-tenon-joint: First off, drill a hole the same diameter as your dowel through the outside mortise walls. Remember to remove the tenon before executing this step!

Once the hole is drilled, dry fit the tenon in its place. Then take an awl and mark the center of the hole. Remove the tenon and before drilling it, offset the location of the awl mark you just made, moving the point towards the shoulder slightly. Again with your awl make a new, off-set reference point. Drill through the tenon at this staggered point and re-assemble the pieces dry. You should be able to see down through the holes but will notice they're slightly offset. This is a good thing.

When you're ready, push a draw bore pin or burnisher down through the holes, wedging them tightly together. Remove the pin and hammer a nice wooden dowel home. This slight offset will act as a kind of lever to draw the two pieces even tighter together. If you decide to just add a common dowel with no offset, then you can drill the mortise and tenon at the same time.

One last test fit and we can move on from here. If a project has a lot of mortise and tenon joinery, I'll sometimes chop all of the mortises first and then go back and saw the entire lot of tenons at once. This keeps things consistent and helps to develop a good rhythm when sawing.

Another variation on mortise and tenon joinery is one I like to call a bridal slip or what others may call a simple bridle Joint. This is a simple method (no pun intended) I use for making frame and panel doors. Be it a wooden panel or glass and traditional stick or mullion, I enjoy cutting this joint both mechanically and aesthetically. For larger doors and entryway applications this construction method is simply not an option. However, while composing small understated doors for fine pieces of cabinetry, this method of joinery excels. It's visually appealing

LEFT **Cutting down the cheek of a carefully laid out tenon.**

ABOVE **Dry fitting a tenon into a freshly cut mortise. Checking for square!**

and a delight in a sense when you open a cabinet door revealing the joinery exposed on its inside edges. Seeing the end grain cheek wrap along, squeezing together the long grain sandwich-tongue is kind of ... well, pleasant! So simple yet so telling, it gives another subtle element for people to 'discover' when exploring handcrafted furniture. Again in this example it was a rule of thirds; $\frac{1}{4}$" shoulders with a $\frac{1}{4}$" tenon ... remember, keep it simple stupid!

Lay out the joint as we did before with nice deep scribe lines. Then cut down to the shoulders using your favorite rip saw, in this case I used a Japanese Dozuki; I found it to be a more refined tool for making these long delicate cuts. Follow this with a quick pair of cross cuts, splitting that tiny scribe line still laying across at the proper shoulder height. Square to the board face I repeat the same sawing techniques as before, beginning at the far side of the tenon in relation to my body, I'll establish a shallow kerf along the face trying my best to walk the line straight clear through.

Once this is accomplished you only need to worry about holding the saw properly and with that wiggly-arm, drunken man dance pull the Dozuki towards you. With the slightest touch and as little force as you can commit, let the saw do what it was naturally intended to do; swiftly cut a straight line down through some hard wood. Enjoy the process and consider what you're doing. Try to get a real sense of your body moving, your arm's elevation in direct relation to your workbench, the wrist and fingers merely guiding, almost a quiet suggestion for the blade to follow the kerf down through the fiber.

As you reach your original vertical saw kerf, concentrate on finishing this new cross cut horizontally square to the first. This will keep

A simple joint used for frame and panel doors. The slip or bridle joint.

Tenon roughly cut with Japanese pull saw. Notice how the saw marks varies from cutting straight across the grain to an angled cut where it meets the outer edges.

Paring away the Dozuki scars left behind while sawing the tenon's cheek.

things in a healthier state when moving on through to our next steps. It may also keep things visually copacetic; seeing the remains of over-cut saw kerfs that didn't seem to have a destination or a purpose is distressing when viewing a completed piece of 'joinery on display' style cabinetry.

At this point I'll take a freshly honed paring chisel and remove those tiny scars left behind in the Dozuki wake. Acknowledge the half scribe you so cleverly split while sawing ... you can still see the saw line right? If not, well, now you know that you no longer have a reference

point so tread lightly while paring. Those who have an entire scribe line with a little extra 'meat' still hanging on, you can bring it all the way down to the scribe line. And those of you whose wood working takes place in an ideal world and all you are left with is a perfect half of the original scribe line ... carry on as if you're normal and please let me know what the weather is like over there!

Once the tenon is complete we can cut out the open mortise. This essentially looks exactly the same as the tenoned piece and should be scribed at the same time as the other. It'll have two crisp lines set in

With the sides of the open mortise sawn, get ready to start chopping.

Starting just shy of the end, begin chopping out the waste material.

Starting just shy of the scribe line, finish squaring the mortise end.

A completed bridal slip with glass panel in walnut. Notice the sides have been planed down to a narrower thickness than the lower door rail and a small bead detail has been hand scratched across the bottom. These small details can add a lot of subtle, visual interest in a simple piece.

¼" from the edges. This time however, instead of cutting the outside cheeks off we'll be concentrating on the interior opening. Keep this in mind and keep the saw blade on the waste side of the scribe lines.

Cut down both sides and get ready to put away the hand saw and grab your ¼" mortising chisel. I'll hold my work piece in the tail vise and start just shy of the end, take my chisel and begin removing the waste.

I'll hold my chisel so the bevel side is facing me; this makes quick work of cleaning out the waste

material. Be sure to take small 'bites' and only chop down about a third of the way through. Continue chopping and moving back, chop a little and move back again towards the mortise bottom. Once you reach your scribe line, turn your chisel around so the bevel is facing away from you and place the tip of the chisel directly into the scribe. Holding the chisel as square as you can chop down and establish the bottom. If you find you're having a difficult time keeping the chisel square, try clamping a small square

or block of wood to the workpiece, just below the bottom scribe line. This will act as a visual reference and help keep your cut true and vertical. Once you have one side cleaned out, flip the piece over and repeat. Go easy when you break down through the waste so you don't bury your chisel into your bench top. Clean up the interior and try a test fit.

Again a nice hand fit is what we're after. If it's too loose, try the shim tick, if it's too tight; plane a little off of each side of the tenon until adequate.

THE PROJECTS

FROM THE CABINETMAKER'S TOOL CHEST to the modern take on a traditional sideboard, the six projects I designed for this book will guide you through some of the more common examples of joinery techniques found in hand-crafted furniture. The pieces themselves will become a small part of your life in the woodshop and then hopefully in your house, your home and your heart for years to come. Building a piece of furniture using only hand tools takes time, patience and determination but is very attainable for everyone interested.

Remember, it's the small details that make a piece look a certain way and can easily be adapted to suit your own styles and tastes. Drawer pulls and wood species alone can really enhance or alter a design. Frame-and-panel or a solid wood door for the wall cabinet? Glass or handmade paper alone will go a long way to making these more your own. Let the book guide you through the process but take liberties where you see fit.

Before you sharpen up those irons and start making shavings I'll mention a few steps I feel are vital when building furniture from a design or plan. First off, decide on the piece you'd like to start with. I tried to introduce them in an order that makes the most technical sense; developing skills, confidence and new techniques as you go. Each project in the sequence offered should prove more of a challenge than the previous ... this is a good thing.

When you decide to begin a project I strongly suggest you read through the entire chapter first; acknowledging each step and taking into account the specific joinery required. Try to visualize the finished piece and study the photos, diagrams and text. Even while I was building these pieces I found it extremely useful to sketch out the designs again and again ... getting a good visual sense of where every component falls and how each part is joined to the next.

If you hit some hurdles along the way, or would just like to discuss the design as a whole, I welcome you to contact me with any questions or concerns. I hope you have fun with these six pieces and when you have them in your own home please let me know; I'd love to hear about them.

Cheers!

OPPOSITE **Six of six ... I wanted to include this shot of all the projects so you could get a better sense of scale between them. Photographs and sizes of furniture can sometimes be deceiving.**

Going Down the Road: A Cabinetmaker's Tool Chest

WHEN I THINK OF A TOOL CHEST I THINK of a carpenter's box, usually open and inviting, a little rough perhaps but clearly made from the hand ... think of Roy Underhill merrily skipping over the stream ... remember the tool box he was carrying? It could be as straightforward as butt joints and nails or elaborate as dovetails and tenons. This book is about building designs with only hand tools, so what I've come up with are both practical and traditional in construction. Well, sort of ...

I've built a few tool box designs and have carried a few tool boxes around at arms length. I still walk with a limp from that cherry monolith I made last year to transport my tools from Cape Breton to Ontario.

Do you need to carry tools? Are you going to be on a job site outside of your workshop? This

chest will be manageable and hold most of your workshop essentials while incorporating some rather unique and practical design elements. For starters the sliding lid, (captured in dadoes) that pushes off the back and is held open to access the interior. While in the open position the lid serves as a shield to cover your two backsaws that are safely held on the exterior back with a protective shelf underneath them. This turns into a little shelf to place things like tiny screws you'd surely loose on-site if you didn't have such a dedicated area to toss them. It has a built in shooting board, work space complete with surface clamp and miter hook that'll get all of

OPPOSITE **Hard maple from Cape Breton and black walnut off cuts from my last commission, this tool chest will hold a surprising amount of hand tools and features some real handy, 'on the road' benefits.**

ABOVE RIGHT **Back panel of tool chest, here you can see the back saw holders, the shooting board on top and the cam clamps in place. When we get to our destination these will hold the chest down to a surface while we're working.**

the applause from your fellow craftsmen on site. I know how many
times I've been installing a cabinet
or perhaps some finish moulding
somewhere ... and a make shift
bench surface, saw hook and shooting board would have been really
handy as well as resting your arse
on the edge from time to time.
Simple in form, as a tool chest
should, we'll get started with the
basic box so we can get on to some
of those unique design elements.

THE CARCASS

Whether you're using four wide
planks or joining up some narrower widths, assemble the four
main carcass components after
working up your cutting list from
the illustrations (yes, it's an important part of the process!). Those
pieces are the front, back and the
two ends, or sides, if you will. The
front corner joinery will be through
dovetails with the back being a
tenon housed in a stopped dado.
The sides will continue past the
chest back, creating a kind of shelf
location where two backsaws will
live. Following the through dovetail
procedure in described in Chapter

Preparing to lay out the joinery for the four main carcass pieces.

3, lay out, cut and dry fit the front to
the side pieces.

To create this 'staggered' or
'broken' dovetail pattern I laid the
entire width of the pieces out as
per normal and then simply refrain
from cutting out the center tail after
marking. When you scribe the tail
board over to the pins it'll be business as usual. This break creates

some visual interest and actually
saves you time in construction! If all
is well in dovetail land we can disassemble, mark and scribe the interior
dado to house the back panel tenon.

You can see the $1/2$" mortise
chisel I'll be using to chop out the
remainder of the mortise once I
remove the bulk of the waste with a
brace and bit and large router plane.

ABOVE Dry fitting the front to side joinery.

RIGHT A deep scribe line will establish the edges of the interior dadoes.

I'll begin with the router plane set to a very fine shaving; this will create the small shoulders needed before I start drilling. A ½" auger bit can sometimes shred a little wood at the surface when beginning a hole. A Forstner bit would be another safe way to begin the dado. Maybe you'd prefer using a paring chisel or back saw? There will always be more ways too skin a ...

From here it's drilling time; a ½" auger bit and my favorite brace make quick work of the waste.

ABOVE **Match your joinery sizes to your tools whenever possible.**

LEFT **Light passes are first taken with a router plane. This will help to eliminate tear out.**

BELOW **Use your drill bit of choice to remove the majority of the waste material.**

With my Dozuki I establish the dadoes depth.

A stopped dado. If you look closely you can see the transition between the mortise chisel dado and that of the small plough plane.

Once again, remove the bulk of the waste with brace and bit. This is the dado for the sliding hinge in the lid.

A router plane completes the dado and cleans up the bottom.

Once I have the bulk of the waste removed I like to take my Japanese Dozuki, (yes, I said pull saw ... this is one application where a Western style saw would not be appropriate) and by laying the saw plate in the narrow shoulder of the stopped dado, draw the saw back towards me and begin establishing the depth of the dado. Again this is just something I like to do to help with tearout and could easily be accomplished with a wide chisel.

Once you get close to your finished depth, remove the rest of material with the mortise chisel. Clean up the bottom again with the router plane and call it done. In the outside edges of the tool box back cut a corresponding tongue or tenon with either a skew block plane or rabbet plane. Another dry fit and we'll cut the stopped dadoes for the bottom panels.

Because we're using through dovetails here, the bottom dado needs to be stopped so it doesn't show up in the outside end grain. You could let it, this being a toolbox but I'm going to take the extra steps to cut stopped dadoes. Lay out the dado and starting at one corner, chop out a mortise by hand. This will give the end of your plough plane somewhere to go when beginning. Now with my plough plane, I can safely cut the dado.

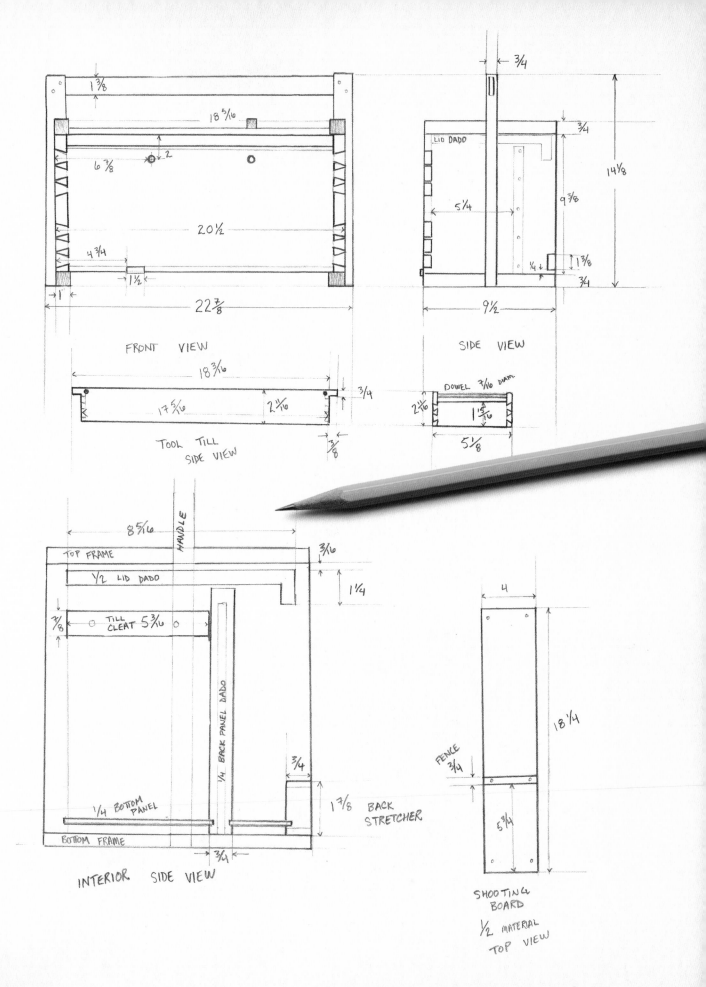

1 3/8

18 5/16

6 7/8   2

20 1/2

4 3/4

1 1/2

1"

22 7/8

FRONT   VIEW

3/4

LID DADO

3/4

5 1/4   9 3/8

14 1/8

1/4   1 3/8

3/4

9 1/2

SIDE   VIEW

18 3/16

17 5/16   2 11/16

3/4

TOOL   TILL
SIDE   VIEW

3/8

DOWEL 7/16 DIAM.

2 11/16   1 15/16

5 1/8

8 5/16   HANDLE

TOP FRAME

3/16

1/2 LID DADO

1 1/4

7/8   TILL
CLEAT 5 3/16

1/4 BACK PANEL DADO

3/4

1/4 BOTTOM PANEL

1 7/8   BACK
STRETCHER

BOTTOM FRAME

3/4

INTERIOR   SIDE VIEW

4

FENCE
3/4

18 1/4

5 3/4

SHOOTING
BOARD

1/2 MATERIAL
TOP VIEW

Roto Hinge

I purchased these 'Roto' hinges years ago for a project and they were sold in a bag of 6. I figured they'd come in handy some day and this lid design is the perfect application. Make sure the dado is deep enough to let the hinge travel its full distance. Cut the lid to size and drill the corresponding holes. A dry fit and test run will be next.

A 'Roto Hinge' will hold the top lid in place and allow it to travel freely, holding it in place again at the back while in the open position. A corresponding hole set back from the front edge of the lid will hold the hinge and lid in place.

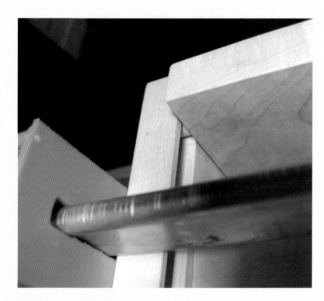

A dry fit. Hinge and dado detail.

Lid travels off the back...

Once the lid travels past the back panel it'll swing down to rest in the vertical position.

You can see the lid stops at this point; I will disassemble the tool chest and lengthen the 'L' shaped dado so, when open, the lid will be flush with the top of the sides.

INTERIOR COMPONENTS

Before I disassemble I'll measure, cut and fit the interior cleats that will hold the till inside. This is also a good time to double check the size of the bottom panel and mark out the dovetail for the back stretcher.

The Till

Assemble the pieces needed for the till. I used some poplar I had in my shop for awhile, and this lightweight wood will help to keep the tool box lighter. Cut the two side pieces to length then measure and cut out the shoulders that will hang off of the interior cleats. A nice snug fit here is what were after. It'll be dovetailed shortly and when we trim our tails it will be shortened ever so slightly for a perfect fit.

I'm using through dovetails for the till but didn't want to go through the trouble of cutting stopped dadoes for the bottom. This is kind of a neat method for through dovetail construction without having to go through the steps of stopped dadoes. Ironically enough I first saw Roy Underhill build a tool chest a few years back and he used this helpful method.

Assemble the till components. The two long sides are already cut to fit, now cut the two ends to size

In this shot you can see the cleat dry fit inside with the two sides cut and fit for the till.

Till components cut with the ends already dovetailed.

Next step is to cut the groove into only the end pieces.

Rip the tails to the depth of the dado.

as well. Begin on the ends with laying out and cutting the tails as you would normally do for any dovetail.

The next step is where this method differs from usual. Take the two short ends and cut the groove for the till bottom. Now before we go ahead and scribe the thickness of the ends onto the two long pieces, we'll rip the sides off of the tails at the same depth as the newly cut dado creating a thinner version.

Next, with our tails ripped and cross cut to width with the waste removed, we can go ahead and transfer this new thickness to the long sides of the till. Once scribed we'll transfer the tails over to the pin board using our usual methods.

PHOTOS AT RIGHT **Close up of above shot. Could it be we're all starring into the face of R.H. Davis himself?**

This antique backsaw manufactured by R.H. Davis Co. came from Mark at Techno primitives. He fully restored it and sent it my way a few months back. Could this explain why he sent it to me so freely? After seeing the photo my wife suggested we Google the name ... this was one of the first photographs we found with the name Davis ... Believe?

Cross cut to remove the waste. Note: Does anyone else see what appears to be a 'face' in the side of my saw plate in this shot?

End pieces ready for next step.

With tails scribed, cut out the pins. Now we don't have to worry about the dadoes showing on the outside of the finished till. Cut the dado to the full length of the front and back till components.

Measure and cut the till bottom panel. In this case I used a solid piece of walnut I had re-sawn a few months back. It's also a good time to round over the top edges of the till sides and pre-drill for the dowels which get set into the inside ends. These will act as handles and will make it much easier to pick the full till up from inside the tool chest. A dry fit and we're ready to glue. I didn't put any finish on mine, deciding to leave it in its natural state.

With the interior components completed I'll measure, mark and cut out the dovetails for the back bottom stretcher. This piece is also rebated using the same, 'no-stop rabbet' method of cutting the tail, plough out the bottom panel groove and then rip the tail to width essentially cutting off the grooves shoulders. Scribe the tail to the side panels and cut the socket. I decided to add a decorative bead to the stretcher as well as the top and bottom of the front panel. Taking only a few minutes of time it again ads another small visual element and helps to elevate a simple tool chest from ordinary to something the grand kids will fight over in fifty years!

Measure and cut the bottom panels and give everything another good going over. With that, it'll be time to spread some glue.

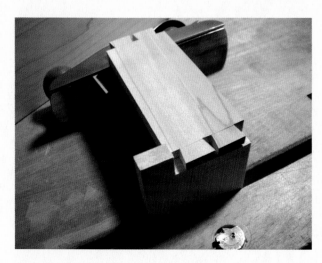
Transferring the tails over to the pin board.

With the pins cut we can now go ahead and plane the groove into the pieces.

Assembled; the dowels acts as handles when removing the till from inside the chest.

Some glue and clamp for a few hours.

Lower frame joinery detail.

Cutting the joinery in the frame and handle pieces.

Exterior Frame and Handle

I'm again using some walnut off cuts and building a kind of cradle that'll capture the ends and transfer the weight through the handle, down the sides and underneath, to help pick up some of the weight of the finished tool box.

With two bottom runners cut to length I'll cut and chisel a small open mortise that will house the stub tenon at the bottom of the two side uprights. This will be glued and screwed using some cast bronze screws left over from my boat building days. This type of hardware is great for any application that may see moisture, like the bottom of a tool chest. These will surely withstand the elements. Some straightforward half-lap joints at the top of the chest sides and a through mortise-and-tenon for the handle.

When all of the frame joinery is to your liking, disassemble and give everything a good going over with a smoothing plane. Glue and re-assemble. When dry I'll drill and install some dowels through the tenons and runners to lock everything in place for good.

The frame components are now ready for assembly.

Shaping one of two cleats that will become back saw holders. These were simply traced from my hand saws and cut out.

Back Saw Holders

The back saw holders are cut from maple scraps left over from the construction process. I used my bow saw to shape them and some file and rasp work to finish. These will be screwed to the back along with a small block holding two inset rare earth magnets. The backsaws simply fit over the custom-shaped cleats and grab the magnets, holding everything in place for our adventures on down the road.

Hold Downs

When we get to our destination or job site we sometimes need to hold our work. Anyone who's actually been at a client's home trying to saw a board or dress an edge on their kitchen counter or coffee table will know this is awkward to say the least. Instead, we'll make some custom bench top appliances suited for this scale of work. Once at our job site the first thing you'll do is clamp the tool chest to a table or counter top ... this is done with our two wooden cam-clamps that'll live in front of the backsaws on our rear panel. A couple of little blocks glued in place will be plenty enough to hold them while en route.

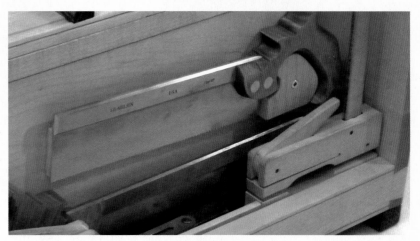

Here you can see the back saw holders in place, keeping the saw safely in place.

The front panel gets two ³/₄" holes drilled through to secure a surface clamp, bench dog or wooden dowel. The small lip or shelf at the bottom edge is to place the heel of a board being worked on ... the right side of this little shelf is in line with the left side of the surface clamp when installed.

When you clamp any work piece to the front panel vertically, you simply move the lower corner over to the right side of the shelf and you'll know your work piece is being held square.

With the surface clamp mounted in one of the front holes and a ¾" wooden dowel in the other, I can edge joint a board up to 24" long!

Now onto the lid and front; Drill a few ¾" holes in your nice new tool box. Don't worry, these will turn this pretty little tool chest into an on-site, table top workbench!

The front two holes are used in conjunction with a surface clamp, bench dog or simply, a wooden dowel. For vertical work holding applications I also cut and shaped a little shelf or lip that provides somewhere for the end of a board to sit while clamped to the front panel. This small maple shelf receives a rabbet and then is glued and screwed. I positioned it so when you

go to clamp a board in the left hole, you simply move the board's bottom right edge over flush with the right edge of the shelf. This will tell you your work piece is square. Perfect for cutting those on-site dovetails.

On site edge jointing? Again, no worries. Clamp your workpiece horizontally into the left side hole and rest the opposite end on a bench dog or dowel installed in the right side. This is why we clamped our box down when we began.

Now onto the miter hook and shooting board. Anywhere on the top walnut stretchers that feels the

most comfortable to you, carefully mark and crosscut down leaving a nice square saw kerf to act as a make shift miter box on site. I only put a 90° in mine on the front left side but you could easily add a couple of 45 degrees or whatever common miter you make. Now that we've crosscut our work piece to length we'll need to shoot the end. What's that? An On-the-Job shooting board attachment? Cool ...

Measure, cut and square up a thin piece of stock suitable for a shooting board. Drill and glue four dowels into the bottom corners and

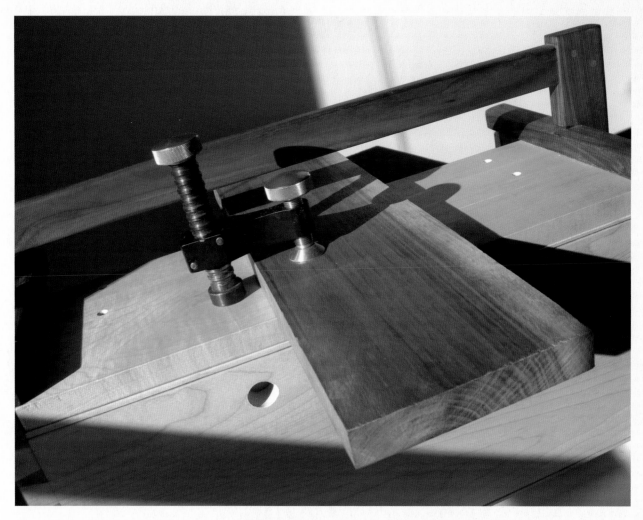

With the shooting board removed, the top serves as another work-area.

when dry cut them so they're in the ¼" ballpark. Drill four corresponding holes into the top of the lid giving these a nice countersink. This will make placement easier for you. The fence is screwed in place, up from the bottom, making sure it's perfectly square to the ramp side. When you're not using the board it can stay put there on top or when you need the surface lid space for other work-holding needs it can be stored on the back shelf in front of the back saws.

A mixture of oil and varnish for the outside and we can call this first project done. Congratulations, you now have somewhere to keep your essential, on-site hand tools and a great little workbench for out-of-shop work.

Shooting a small edge on the tool chest. Remember to only use a No. 4 size plane for this application. Anything larger and you'll constantly be running into the frame components at each end. Here I'm using my James Krenov smoothing plane.

'Ain't No Feathers Around Here Boys...'

FIRST THINGS FIRST WE SHOULD TRY TO think of this little cabinet as a straightforward drawer hanging on the wall. With half-blind dovetails at one end, (that being the top) and through dovetails at the other, a drawer in essence is what this cabinet is. A sliding-dovetailed center divider and two solid wood drawers will sharpen your dovetailing skills and in my case make a nice little place for my wife to store tea bags. If you're still getting comfortable in the dovetailing process, this project will really push you forward and you'll be a dovetailing guru in no time at all. Let's begin ...

Preparing Your Stock

Because the overall size of this piece is small, take your time and choose some really nice wood. Any time I'm able to use one solid plank for a door, I go out of my way to make it stand out. A more subtle door design could be a simple frame and panel. You could easily incorporate your favorite door style into this piece but here I'm using the rest of my walnut and wanted it to make a statement.

For the interior drawers I chose a nice little scrap of birds-eye maple and another small plank of purple heart I purchased for $8 from a local lumber yard off-cut pile. These will really contrast each other but somehow work as a whole within the walnut case and frame. Kind of a 'crafty or whimsical' feel that makes me smile when I open it. My two-year-old daughter seems to approve and has already laid claim, so the pleas-

ant, inviting feel of the piece is not just in my imagination. The purple heart had to be re-sawn so with my restored rip saw I made the cut.

ABOVE **Begin by cross cutting your carefully selected wood.**

The purple heart is hard and dense; it takes a few minutes and a bit of muscle to get down through. The small wedge helps to keep the kerf open as I go.

With my cut list laid out before me, and all my pieces square on six sides and planed smooth, I start off shaping the top and bottom pieces. Mark the curve and clamp the pieces together in your vise. Shape them simultaneously to keep continuity in profile. This curve was made by eye with a quick pencil line and a bent baton of hardwood.

A low-angle block plane followed by a spokeshave, and the gentle arch is quickly achieved. The grain in this walnut was straight and clean; a real pleasure to work with hand tools. Once I have these to where I want them, I'll get the side panels ready and lay things out on my bench top.

From this point on we're essentially making a drawer right? Cut the back dado that'll hold the cabinet's dust panel and get ready to lay out and cut the dovetails. I used the same 'skip tail' layout I used in the front of the tool chest. You'll notice as you work through these designs I often use a handful of aesthetic elements in my pieces. Find some that work for you and try incorporating them into your own pieces. These will add a sense of individuality and show people that this is your work!

Once you have the half-blind and through dovetails all cut, try doing a dry fit. If all is well, lay out the knife hinge mortise placement and mark out the interior framing. Disassemble and get ready for the sliding dovetail.

For the main interior drawer divider I'm using a sliding dovetail; you could easily get away with a mortise and tenon or perhaps some dowels. Being as this design is a lesson in dovetails I'm going with that.

Measure, cut and shoot the divider, being sure to allow extra length for the dovetails. I have a dedicated dovetail plane that'll make quick work of this step but if you don't have one, you can scribe and with a back saw and using a wood block as a guide, achieve the same results. Clean up the inside edges with a chisel.

BELOW **Shaping the cabinet top and bottom together will help maintain continuity between the pieces.**

Lay out the pieces to re-evaluate the final cabinet dimensions.

Cutting the sliding dovetail in the center drawer divider with a dedicated dovetail plane manufactured by ECE in Germany.

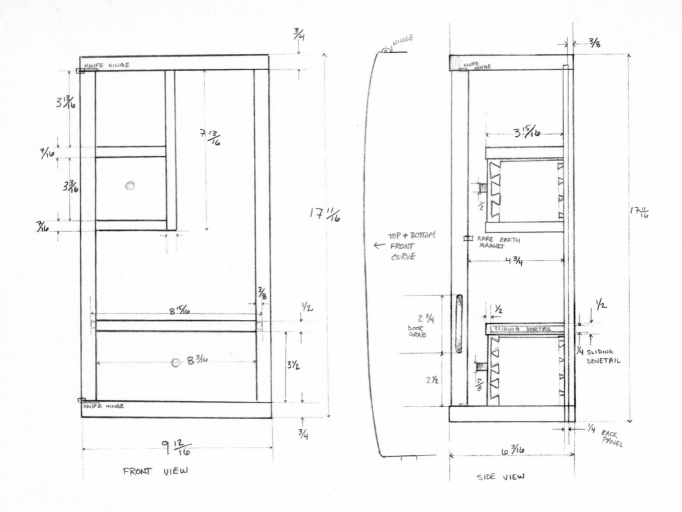

KNIFE HINGE

3 13/16
7/16
3 3/16
7/16

7 13/16

17 11/16

3/4

3/8
8 15/16
1/2

8 3/16

3 1/2

KNIFE HINGE

9 12/16
3/4

FRONT VIEW

HINGE
KNIFE HINGE

3/8

3 15/16

1/2

TOP & BOTTOM
← FRONT
CURVE

RARE EARTH
MAGNET

4 3/4

17 11/16

2 3/4
DOOR
GRAB

2 1/2

1/2
SLIDING DOVETAIL
5/8

1/2
1/4 SLIDING
DOVETAIL

1/4 BACK
PANEL

6 3/16

SIDE VIEW

When complete, scribe and cut out the interior groove. Again, nice deep scribe lines and with a back saw, then chisel. You should have no trouble removing the waste. This isn't really a tapered sliding dovetail but I'll tend to widen the back end slightly with a chisel to aid in assembly.

Mark out the top drawer assembly and get those pieces ready. Because this top drawer is so light and on such a small scale, oak dowels and butt joints are all that's required. I use a self-centering jig to first drill the 1/4" holes in the pieces. Then I'll insert these center-finding pins and on my bench top, press the pieces together. The small dimples left behind will show me exactly where to drill my corresponding dowel holes. This is a great example of modern

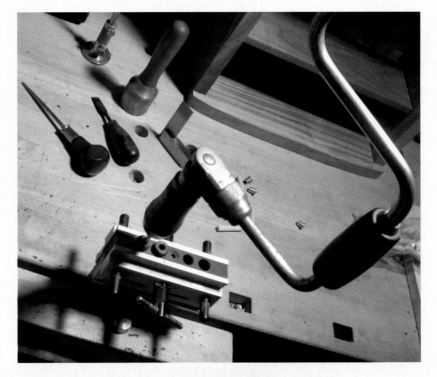

A doweling jig with brace and bit work well together in the hand tool shop.

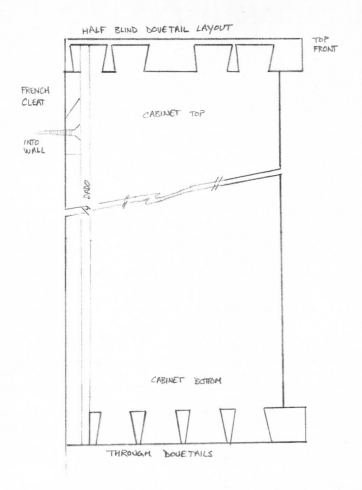

HALF BLIND DOVETAIL LAYOUT

TOP FRONT

FRENCH CLEAT

INTO WALL

DADO

CABINET TOP

CABINET BOTTOM

THROUGH DOVETAILS

Working Wood

*finger joint and dovetail went
out walkin' through the wood …
cursing all the alders!*

*"ain't no crows feet over here
boys…"*

*plane the grain through tapered
flame cathedrals in the aspen*

*working wood like joseph could,
communion in the end grain
chamfer down…*

*unplugg the drill and wrap
your hand around the word of
working man*

*'round the word of working
man…*

day tool conveniences, while mostly
marketed to the power tool user, the
dowel centers can be a great help in
the hand tool work shop!

Once all of the pieces are drilled,
glue in your dowels and let dry. Cut
to length and try another dry fit.

**Another 'modern convenience' being employed … dowel centers mean no measuring involved
so less chance of error creeping in.**

With the basic carcass complete we'll cut our door stock to size and while holding it in place, scribe into its' top, the cabinet's profile. Remove and plane down to these lines with hand planes, spoke-shaves, scrapers and sand paper. Whatever works until you have a nicely rounded, convex door. Cut the mortises for the knife hinges and assemble your stock for the drawers and cabinet back.

I made the two drawers in my usual way, half-blind in the front with through dovetails in the back. The bottoms and main cabinet back panel are all solid wood that was re-sawn by hand here in my shop a few months ago. It was given lots of time to cure specifically for this project. The delicate size of the drawer components may challenge some but follow the dovetailing procedures described earlier and take your time. Nothing has changed except the scale of the work. People generally see a small cabinet like this one and think it would be quite easy to build. This is simply not the case ... I find some of these smaller scale designs much harder to execute than larger work.

ABOVE **The door shaped and installed. With the interior close to complete, a light coat of oil is applied.**

RIGHT **A rare earth magnet inset into the cabinet's side and door make for a quick door catch.**

‘Tried and True’ oil and varnish blend … a nice product from a nice company.

Some last minute details like a small recess in the lower right edge of the door acts as a pull. This was carved out with a small gouge. The interior drawer pulls are nothing more than dowels that have been drilled and smaller, contrasting dowels inserted. They were intentionally hand drilled off of center reflecting again a kind of whimsical feeling to the piece.

When all is ready, glue things up and finish to your liking. Again as with all of my pieces, a few coats of my favorite oil/varnish mixture! I'll give a piece a rub and then let stand for about an hour. Remove any residue still on the surface and let stand overnight. In the morning a light rub with steel wool and repeat the process. Follow this process until you have the luster you desire. Some of my pieces get two to three coats of finish while others can easily get up to seven or eight coats! Especially table tops.

Remember with this type of finishing, the more you rub the better it looks!

Tea anyone?

Skinny Legs and All...

I'VE ALWAYS BEEN A FAN OF SHAKER STYLE FURNITURE; the straight, uncomplicated forms that welcome you in with a glimpse back into an unhurried time. When days seemed to be spent working with hand and in heart, from the past these qualities are reflected in shape.

At first glance, this pleasant side table design may indeed be mistaken for a classic Shaker side table; a Saturday table perhaps, as they're called, because they were generally projects that workers would fabricate at week's end using the off cuts collected through the work days. However, upon closer inspection of this table you'll find Japanese-inspired joinery in the dovetailed 'drawer box'. Three half-blind, dovetailed drawers with solid wood throughout highlight the design. The 'floating' table top helps to give the piece a lighter feel while the aprons and rails reflect an Arts and Crafts influence. The gentle tapering legs add another elegant element.

We'll use no less than six different joints, all cut and made by hand. Perhaps this made-by-hand element reflects more the true Shaker influence emerging from the design rather than its simple silhouette. This project is sure to challenge the builder and delight its owner. Let's begin ...

THE TOP LEG-TO-APRON JOINT; A HOUSED DOVETAIL BRIDAL SLIP?

Establish the cut list and clearly label all of the components; use a cabinetmakers triangle where applicable. We'll start with the legs, those four skinny legs, and lay out all of the joinery.

Following the diagrams on the following pages, carefully scribe with a marking knife all of the mortises on each of the legs. Now beginning at the top, we'll start off with one of the more challenging joints to execute; the housed, dovetail-with-dado at the top of each leg where they join the front and back aprons. Ironically this joint is pretty well hidden from view when completed but adds a great deal of strength to the design and eliminates some of the racking forces on a small side table like this one.

With a small square and knife, sharp pencil and good lighting; mark off the width of the shoulders all around the apron ends. Follow by scribing the depth across the piece for the dovetail and lower shoulders. Mark some X's in the waste area so we don't cut on the wrong side of our scribe lines (photo, top)!

Place each piece vertically in your vise and rip saw the outer corner down to the end of the dovetail line. Turn the piece horizontally and cross cut to finish. You should be left with something that looks like the middle photo. Now cut the underside shoulder of the dovetails bottom off. (Bottom photo.)

With a small bevel gauge or dovetail marker, mark out the cut lines for the tapered sides of the dovetail and with a large chisel gently tap down some nice deep registration marks.

The layout. Add some X's to identify the waste piece.

First steps, the corner notch is removed with a rip and then a cross cut.

Cut off the lower shoulder, next.

Dog down the piece horizontally to your bench and carefully pare down to these lines. Take light passes and remove the waste as you go. This step will determine one side or 'slope' of the dovetail. Clean up any waste; strive for nice square corners and edges. Turn the piece over and tackle the other side. Repeat for the second apron and you should have four joints that look like the photo below, right.

With our housed dovetails all cut out we can transfer these over to the tops of the legs. Carefully place the apron across the top of the legs where they'll be living. Take a knife and mark out the dado width and depth.

LEFT **Establishing the sides of the housed dovetail. This is approximately a 1:7 degree slope.**

One side established.

One of the apron-to-leg joints complete.

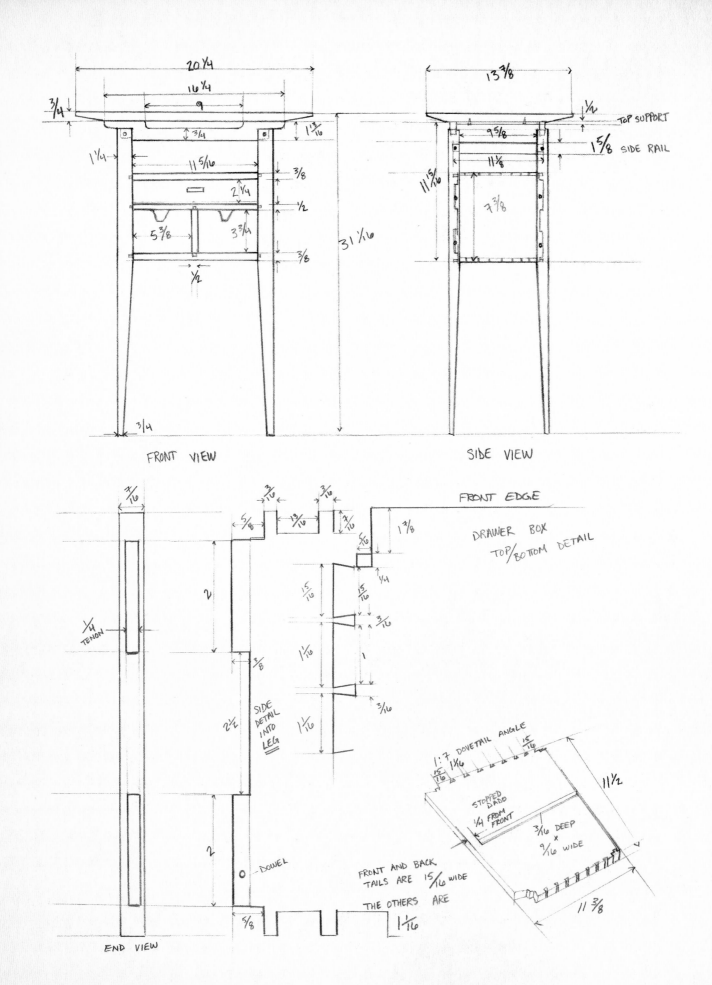

20 1/4

16 1/4

9

3/4

3/4

1 3/16

1 1/4

11 5/16

3/8

2 1/4

1/2

5 3/8   3 3/4

3/8

1/2

31 1/16

3/4

FRONT VIEW

13 7/8

TOP SUPPORT

1/2

9 5/8

1 5/8 SIDE RAIL

11 1/8

11 15/16

7 3/8

SIDE VIEW

7/16

3/16   3/16

5/8   1 3/16

7/16

FRONT EDGE

1 7/8

DRAWER BOX
TOP/BOTTOM DETAIL

1/4 TENON

2

3/8

5/16

1/4

15/16   15/16

3/16

1 1/16   1

SIDE DETAIL INTO LEG

2 1/2

3/16

1 1/16

2

DOWEL

5/8

1 1/16

1:7 DOVETAIL ANGLE   15/16

15/16   1 1/16

STOPPED DADO
1/4 FROM FRONT

11 1/2

3/16 DEEP
×
9/16 WIDE

FRONT AND BACK
TAILS ARE 15/16 WIDE

THE OTHERS ARE   1 1/16

11 3/8

END VIEW

First shallow cuts in the leg top.

ABOVE **Cleaning out the waste.**

LEFT **Carefully chopping out the waste.**

With a rip back saw, cut down to the shallow top shoulder lines being very careful not to over cut; this would show up in the finished piece and would be there to remind you every time you look at the table when completed.

With a very sharp bench or paring chisel, clean out the waste. Notice in the top right photo how I have my left fingers and thumb wrapped around the top of the leg and pressing down on the back of the chisel. This allows for small, controlled cuts through the end grain of the ash wood.

Now we focus on cutting out the dovetail socket, following the same procedure we do for any blind dovetail; cutting down into the waste area of the socket at a 45° slope establishing the sides of the housing. Next it's chisel time to remove the waste and clean up the corners.

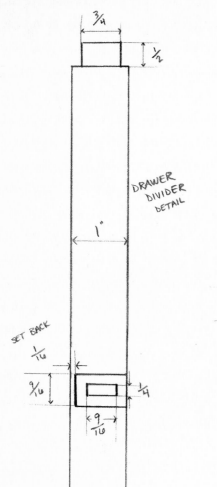

DRAWER DIVIDER DETAIL

3/4

1/2

1"

SET BACK 1/16

9/16

1/4

9/16

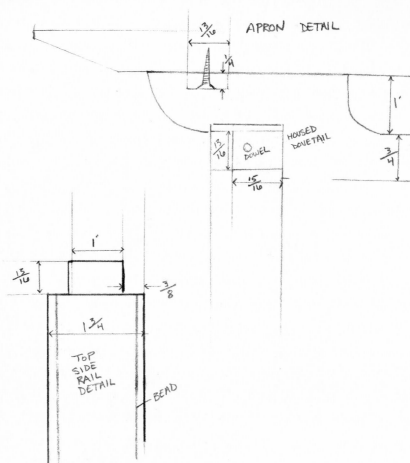

APRON DETAIL

13/16

1/4

13/16

DOWEL

HOUSED DOVETAIL

15/16

1'

3/4

1"

13/16

3/8

1 3/4

TOP SIDE RAIL DETAIL

BEAD

Before dry fitting the pieces I like to cut a very shallow chamfer into the bottom of the dovetail, this will help things along when assembling the components.

Fit and finished ... happy? Great, set aside and we'll move on from here. What's that? One out of the four legs to apron joints are loose? No time like the present to address this! A loose fitting joint should require no more fussing than a couple of thin shims glued to the sides of the dovetail. I say two shims because placing a single shim on one side could offset the fit even more. Rip out a couple of thin strips from the scrap pile of ash you have over there in the corner, and glue a couple on. When it has fully cured, gently pare down until you have that perfect fit we were trying so hard for in the first place!

A slight bottom chamfer on the dovetail will aid in assembly and give somewhere for the glue to go.

Cutting some thin shims to beef up any ill-fitting joints; these four cuts ate up an eighth of an inch in total from my scrap pile, and yes these cuts were done with a hand saw!

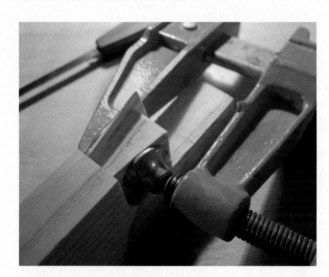

Reality check: a loose fitting joint is cured

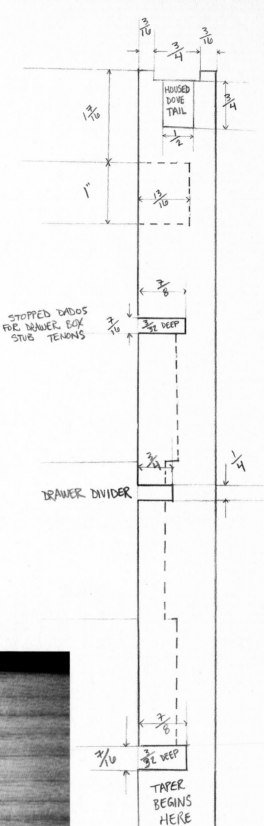

HOUSED DOVE TAIL

STOPPED DADOS FOR DRAWER BOX STUB TENONS

$\frac{3}{32}$ DEEP

DRAWER DIVIDER

$\frac{3}{32}$ DEEP

TAPER BEGINS HERE

LEFT **Dry-fitting the joint.**

With the leg to apron joints complete I'll slide on down and mark out the front to back rail mortise as well as the long haunched mortises the drawer box sides will fit in. Because these are full length, we'll divide the tenons in two, creating a double tenon. Carefully lay out the mortise and again with brace and bit, remove the bulk of the waste. In the photo at the right, you can see from right-to-left, the different stages of the cut. From drill bit to bench chisel, clean-up the sides of the mortise.

A small router plane establishes a consistent depth of the two elevations. To complete the mortise, a ¼" mortise chisel squares the ends and finishes the pocket while my swan neck comes in handy here as well.

With the top of the legs and front-to-back joinery complete, focus on the inside leg mortises which will house the drawer divider and box.

Lay these out in the same way as before and gently remove the small bits of material. These are delicate joints that should be carefully executed. Slamming hammers and jamming irons will only lead to frustrating results come time for assembly. Consider each process and remember to keep your blades sharp; I used a paring chisel and small router plane for the four slots that will accept the front edges of the drawer box top and bottom.

RIGHT **Set aside the finished aprons and legs to begin the drawer box.**

Lay out the mortises down each leg and begin by removing the bulk of the waste with a brace and bit. Then finish off by hand with some chisel and router plane work.

Establishing the depth of the grooves for the drawer box.

The Drawer Box

Take your drawer box pieces and if need be, clean up any glue joints, clamp marks and/or other undesirable blemishes. Smooth down to a good finished stage. If you have some wider stock and can get your panels from one piece you may want to consider that and adapt for some seasonal wood movement. I needed to joint a couple of narrower boards together so I'll begin after the glue clean-up stage.

On the drawer box side pieces lay out some scribe lines for the tenons. Refer between the illustrations here and the mortises you've already cut. The same?

No worries, make the tenons to fit your mortises. Cut out and clean up each until you're happy with a nice dry fit.

Follow this procedure with tackling the side front-to-back rails. By now this closed mortise-to-tenon thing should be second nature right?

A cabinet scraper makes quick work for the glue joint clean up crew.

Drawer box front edge all cut, cleaned and ready to dance.

LEFT A nice dry fit.

ABOVE Another dry fit will assemble all of the components; look for gaps and check for square. Errors will be easier to fix now before we get into the main drawer box body.

Disassemble the pieces and gather up those nice new dovetail tools. It's time to lay out and cut the main drawer box body through dovetails.

Drawer Box Interior

Following your cut list, size the interior components and fit them out, runners, guides and dividers. Disassemble the drawer box to attach the runners, cut the groove for the center divider, plough the rabbet into the back edges for the drawer box dust panel to live, cut the tiny little mortise and tenon joint connecting the horizontal drawer divider to the vertical drawer rail and general interior clean up. Whew! Now we're getting somewhere.

Take into account the shoulders that will mate with the legs-lay these out before you begin marking out the dovetails. The actual dovetail spacing can be as straight forward as you see fit; again, this may be a good spot to add your own artistic embelishments.

After cutting the pins I'll do some fine tuning...

ABOVE **Drawer box dry fit.**

LEFT **Fitting the drawer box to the table legs.**

Shaping the Pieces

I think it's a good time to stop for station identification. Let's disassemble the parts and do some final shaping; a bead in the side rails and some small chamfers on the side tenons and then onto the tapered legs. I suppose you could easily skip this step and leave the legs square; but then again, you wouldn't really be able to call the piece skinny legs and all now would you? Either and all ways are correct, do what feels good!

Lay out some dark pencil lines to establish the starting point of the taper. With the leg held firmly in your tail vise begin to plane down, being careful to stay clear of the tiny island where the taper meets the flat. We want this to be a clean and crisp transition so we'll finely shave it in later on with a block plane. Tapering these small legs can be a pretty quick and relatively stress free venture.

From here we can cut-out the curves and shape the top aprons; I started by establishing the inside curves with a 1" drill bit and then, using my frame saw, I cut out the entire shape. I cleaned things up with a combination of spokeshave, card scrapers and files.

Anywhere you have to use a mechanical fastener on this piece, which should only be where the top attaches to the small cleats; drill these holes now and slightly countersink each side. With a small file, elongate the holes to allow for seasonal movement in the top.

Gather your thoughts and re-assemble one last time before we can start sub-assembly glue ups. This will be your last chance to address any problems or change any design elements either aesthetically or structurally.

Scratching a small bead into the side rails.

Tapering the legs with Jack plane.

With a small hand countersink, countersink both sides of any through fasteners.

A small file elongates the screw holes to allow for seasonal movement in the table top.

Registration cuts will help when planing the bevel on the table top.

Planing the bevel in the table top underside; the saw cuts make for a visual reference when establishing the depth and slope.

The Table Top

With the drawer box and frame of the table complete we can move on to the top and the drawers. If your table top is not yet cut to final dimension do it now. Great, let's cut the bevel on the underside.

When making large bevels like this I'll start off by marking the two edges on the table top bottom and sides. Then, with a fine tooth saw, I make registration cuts down until I just kiss the two outside marks I've made. Make these cuts all around the perimeter with approximately 6" spacing.

Now with a jack plane or jointer, begin beveling the top. Follow down until you can just barely see your saw cuts. Finish off with a smoothing plane or low angle block. I'll also put a small chamfer on the table top edge as well.

Assembly

With all of the components completed (aside from the drawers), we can begin some sub-assemblies. To begin we'll glue up the drawer box making sure to first install the drawer guides on the interior of the two sides. This is where you'll really find out how those dovetailing skills are coming along.

When fully dry it's on to attaching the drawer box to the legs, top rails and aprons. All of those dry fits should really be paying off now. With a small brush to spread the glue into all of these miniature mortises we can strive for a clean and relatively easy assembly.

While I still have the frame clamped up waiting for things to set, I'll drill and install the wooden dowels through the top, front leg-to-apron joint as well as the side drawer box-to-leg joints. There should be three per leg on each side and just the one at the top front. I used a contrasting wood species, in this case walnut, to better show-off the joinery. If this table was for a client and not a demonstration piece for this book, then perhaps I would have used a matching wood to make things a little more subtle.

Frame and drawer box assembled.

Drawers

Again the drawers are made from solid wood with half blind dovetails in the front and through dovetails in the back ... no surprises. The dovetail spacing is up to you!

Drawer Pulls

Well here we are again at the last stages of finishing another piece. Now all there is to decide is what kind of drawer pulls we'll use. Hand made? Store bought? Maybe a simple finger hole drilled into the faces. Maybe a finger hole drilled into the faces and shaped further with files and rasps? Stand back and look at the table you've created. It probably looks pretty similar to the one I made here but it will no doubt have a few of its own characteristics. Make the drawer pulls to suit your own taste; this will bring the piece further from my design and closer to your own. Add some beads to the drawer fronts; maybe you decided not to bevel the table top? What kind of wood did you use? Will you use a simple oil/varnish finish or are you one to stain your work? Whatever you decide should be a reflection of who you are as a woodworker. Develop your own style and add these aesthetic elements to suit your own tastes and décor. Be proud and confident with your own opinions and accomplishments. You just finished another piece of furniture!

These carefully fitted drawers' need some pulls ... the design should be up to you. This is where you really need to throw in your own two cents!

Dovetail spacing through out the three drawers can change like this example or stay consistent between the two lower drawers. Again, it's up to you to decide; after all, it's your table, why not make it truly your own.

Where the Good Books Go?

THIS SMALL BOOKCASE FEATURES THROUGH MORTISE AND tenon joinery, hand-made Japanese paper paneled doors (say that five times fast) and a fine grid work for the mullions, or sticks ... or whatever other word you may regionally use to call those thin dividers that are suspended within the door frames. I never could keep the names straight. The through tenons being the main joinery design, would suggest an Arts and Crafts style while the aesthetic elements and embellishments compliment a more Japanese inspired motif; this is what led to my decision on using the Japanese paper for the door panels. The biggest challenge in this piece will be accurate lay-out to ensure clean visible joints on the through tenons; let's start there.

WOOD PREP AND LAYOUT

Start by getting your cut list together. In my prototype I used some flame birch I had sitting on the wood shelf for a few years, waiting for that perfect design to come along to use the highly figured hardwood. In hindsight, this may not have been the ideal cabinet for this mosaic species; my four year old son has come to call this wood, "lavawood". Through the years I've found the more figured the wood the more difficult it is to work; isn't that the way though, that hidden beauty underneath ... that's the hardest gem to get to. The Birch was no exception and I'll share with you my challenges later on; but for now we'll start by laying out the pieces taking note of the lower small shoulder the doors will eventually sit on. Note the location on the two side panels and rip down to them. A short cross cut to remove the waste, then plane and scrape things smooth. This is the best time to make this long cut and will establish the top and bottom for visual reference from this point on.

From here we can lay out the through mortises and interior dados that will house the top and bottom non-adjustable shelves. Think of it as the frame work.

The top of each side panel will get this same treatment where they meet and eventually pass through the cabinet top, but I started with

Ripping jointed panels to width.

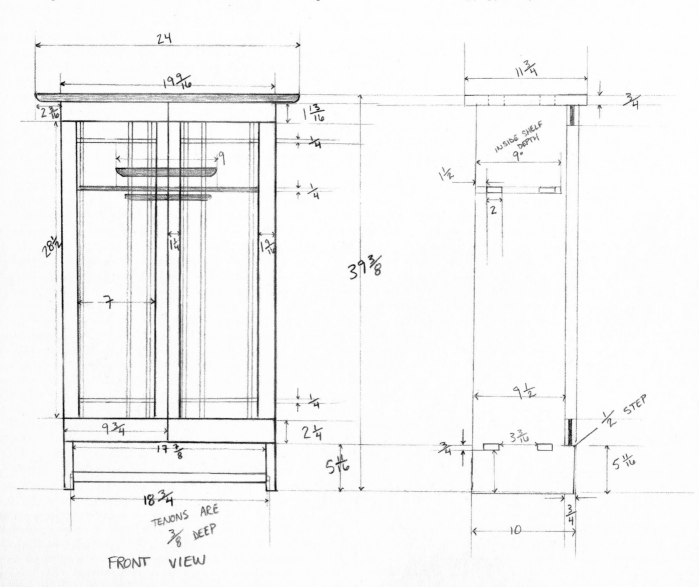

FRONT VIEW

concentrating my efforts here on the interior side panels.

Deep crisp knife lines followed with a tiny 'v' chiseled to the waste side of the lines will help deal with any tearout and show me where things are going.

Once the mortises are chopped through I'll come back with my large router plane and establish the depth of these full dados. Hind sight being twenty-twenty, these could be stopped dados but I was clearly in this 'through joinery' state of mind. The exterior side of the through mortises will also get scribed now.

For through mortises I begin chopping on the inside, or better said, non-show surface, but only go about a third of the way through. Then flip the piece over and from the outside, chop down to meet. Clean and slow, removing little bites of wood will help with any tearing or blow-outs. The birch I'm using is brittle along the wild grains of figure and is already showing signs of its limitations ... or is that me?

My side panels were made from two jointed pieces; if one wide panel is used you may need to address any seasonal wood movement; for a piece this size I would recommend a few jointed boards as opposed to one wide plank. You see antique furniture designs all of the time with wide stable boards that have held together for decades, finely shaped from big, beautiful trees that were once so plentiful around North America. Those trees are hard to find today but if you have some, try it out. If this piece is staying with you in your home as my version will be, then you can take greater risks in your construction options. If I was building the piece for a client, then I would joint up some narrower boards for the added stability on the side panels.

I wouldn't want to be running around all over the country repair-

Accurate lay out is key to well-fitting through tenon joints, be careful here.

Using the mortise as a guide we can transfer accurate lines down through for the tenons.

ing little doors and drawers here and there when the inevitable changes occur in solid wooden furniture and the potential for stuck little drawers and tight little doors become welcoming visits seasonally. Ah now, there could be some reason in using wider planks with the hope that once the piece has left your workshop you'll be able to go visit it and the friendly people who've

adopted it from you. Put on the kettle we'll have a cup of tea. They are always the welcoming ones aren't they? Supporting you and the love of a craft; for now on this prototype as it may be; my own bookcase for my family to enjoy, I can take risks and make design challenges. If it moves, then I will fix it.

Simple enough?

LEFT **Sawing the tenons;
the second scribe line
represents the distance
past the outside of the
side panel the tenon
will pass.**

BELOW **Chopping out
the waste with Japanese
style chisel and a heavy
mallet; this birch is hard
and brittle so I really
had to be careful.**

With all of the mortises cut we
can move on to the tenon layout.
Instead of trying to measure and
mark my tenon positions I'll actually clamp the side panel in my
shoulder vise with the inside facing
out, away from the bench top, and
hold the shelf piece as if it were
being assembled. Now, flip the shelf
piece over, end for end onto the
bench top so the top of the shelf
stock is now upside down. Bring the
two pieces together and locate the
tenons through the mortise. This
will keep the pieces in line for exact
layout position.

When the tenons have been accurately scribed we can start sawing.
These tenons don't have cheeks, so
I'll begin with the vertical rip cuts
and then cross cut down to meet.

With the cross cuts completed
I'll use a fret saw and clear out most
of the waste between the tenons,
then chisel out the remaining wood.
Again, like any chiseling of this
nature, I'll start on the less seen
face and complete the cuts from the
show sides.

With the tenons cut I'll return
my focus to the inside of the side
panels and finish off the dados. My
large router plane will plough out
the hardwood in no time.

With the sides fitting nicely
together with the two fixed cross
shelves I'll take a few hours and let
them get acquainted.

**Routing out the waste in the interior panel dados. This small shoulder will help deal with the
racking forces on the carcass.**

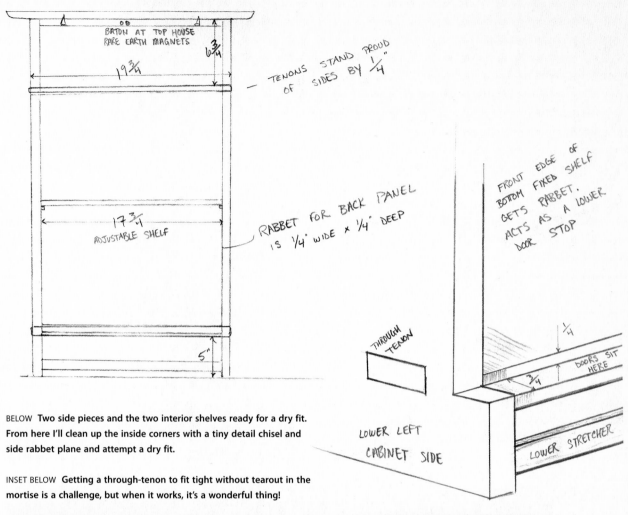

BATON AT TOP HOUSE
RARE EARTH MAGNETS

$6\frac{3}{4}$

$19\frac{3}{4}$

TENONS STAND PROUD
OF SIDES BY $\frac{1}{4}$"

$17\frac{3}{4}$
ADJUSTABLE SHELF

RABBET FOR BACK PANEL
IS $\frac{1}{4}$" WIDE × $\frac{1}{4}$" DEEP

5"

FRONT EDGE OF
BOTTOM FIXED SHELF
GETS RABBET.
ACTS AS A LOWER
DOOR STOP

THROUGH
TENON

$\frac{1}{4}$

DOORS SIT
HERE

$\frac{3}{4}$

LOWER LEFT
CABINET SIDE

LOWER STRETCHER

BELOW Two side pieces and the two interior shelves ready for a dry fit. From here I'll clean up the inside corners with a tiny detail chisel and side rabbet plane and attempt a dry fit.

INSET BELOW Getting a through-tenon to fit tight without tearout in the mortise is a challenge, but when it works, it's a wonderful thing!

Using a solid piece of wide walnut stock for the top. The two smaller pieces, pictured resting on the shelf, will come to be the top rails for the cabinet doors. Maybe some angled concave doors next time?

Walking back into the woodshop and seeing basically a frame standing in front of you is nice. Smile at it and enjoy it while you get some coffee into you before moving on to the top.

I mentioned earlier that the beauty in the birch is this incredible natural flame that's occurring. So I had this stock air drying for two years in my shop back home, then for the past seven months here with me in my new shop, and now finally working it into a project. My moisture level was about 12%, which is damn near perfect in my world, so you'd think things would be stable. Wrong. The top panel I had carefully chosen for the rippled figure had cupped and twisted like a pretzel! Murphy's Law, right? It couldn't have happened to the bottom or back pieces ... no, it was the top. Why? Because it was the one with the most beautiful figure of the whole lot. When I think about it

now, I smile. The real sweet stuff is the hardest to get to. So now what? If this piece was for a client I'd have to talk with them and see how they felt with an aesthetic change in wood species for the top. Another option may be to run out and try to find some flame birch that's dry. Not bloody likely. But wait, this birch was dry ... ah, there lies the rub.

I've decided to use an off-cut of walnut I have in my shop which also appears to be 'dry'. It is flat and it's loaded with figure. The story will be that's why I chose it; to match the highly figured wood from one species to the next! Possible?

I've also decided (seeing as this bookcase will hold most of my wood working library) to use one wide plank. Why not right? This way I'll get to see how much it'll move and what it will do to the joinery of the pieces when and if it does. When you build your own bookshelf you may want to avoid this self-

absorbed, wood movement experiment with the top of a nice piece of furniture. But for the sake of my education and my own George-like curiosity I'm going to use a full-width solid plank. Hey, they did it in the old days. I'll keep you posted on how it goes. Check the Made by Hand site late next summer for an update on:

The Dangerously Wide Walnut Plank I Foolishly Used for the Top of the Flame Birch Book Cabinet.

Following the same procedure you used for the sides, carefully lay out the top mortises. Chop them out and then follow with scribing down through them onto the cabinet sides. Again, saw, fret saw and chop the tenons to a fine fit. This is the top remember, this is what everyone will spill they're drinks on, so make it nice. For the underside of the edges I simply rounded them upwards with my low-angle block plane.

With the top joinery complete, I dry fit again, disassemble and lay out to cut the rabbet in the back of the side panels. This will help to locate the back panel of the cabinet.

Cut the mortises for the lower front stretcher as well. It'll help to keep the sides in place or at the very least add an aesthetic appeal rather than actual construction reinforcement benefits or CRB for short (just kidding.)

Once the mortises are complete you can go ahead and make the stretcher. Cross cut to size, plane the surfaces and cut the tenons.

I decided to give a bit more form to this lower component by shaping it with my spoke shave and card scrapers. You could leave it square or safely eliminate it altogether. The through tenons on the shelves above are more than adequate for structural integrity. It's your bookcase remember?

To recap, we have the two main shelves, the top and two sides and now the lower stretcher complete ... all right, now we can move on to the doors.

I'm using a simple bridal slip for the doors with the upper and lower rails running through horizontally in front of the stile tops. Most builders tend to have the two outside stiles on a door run long but I've always preferred the look of the upper and lower rails being visually longer; that horizontal line appeals to me ... like watching a sunset or better yet, a sunrise. It could also be some form of wood-induced osmosis combined with

staring at Krenov's *The Fine Art of Cabinetmaking* for four years! Man, you don't get tired of that. In this example though I thought it helped the doors stand out, giving an illusion of a wider footprint as a whole to the structure.

Following the same procedure I described in Chapter Three, cut all the joinery for the main door frames.

BELOW **Another dry fit with the lower stretcher installed, then on to the doors.**

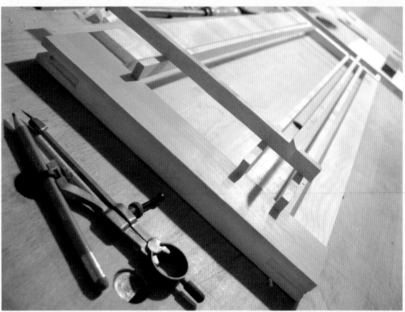

Shaping the lower stretcher.

After dry fitting the door, the 'sticks' are arranged. This was my first impulse, three vertical sticks on the inside and one on the outside. This was later changed because I felt it began to look cluttered over the door's width. Maybe a little too institutionalized?

After a good dry fit we can disassemble the door frames being sure you label everything as you go! With the doors apart, take the two center stiles and plane them down so they finish off about 3/16" thinner than the rest of the door frames.

Cut the rabbets for the panels while things are apart. Stopped rabbets on a frame and panel door shouldn't pose too much of a problem. Clearly scribe your parameters so when the door goes together you don't see the rabbet in the end grain. Seeing as the rails are long and the stiles kept short, we can go ahead and cut a full-length rabbet on the inside edges of the stiles. These will be covered by the rail joint when assembled. The top and bottom rails will have to have stopped rabbets. Deep crisp scribe lines will make this procedure run smoothly. Beginning at an end, we'll need to establish a shallow shoulder; I usually use a chisel and remove the waste or perhaps for wider rabbets I'll pre-drill some holes at each end. With a small plough plane begin taking some fine shavings, being careful not to start your cut on the wrong side of the short rabbet you just cut. Plane down as much as possible and clear away the remaining waste with a router plane or chisel. Once all of the rabbets are cut we'll focus on the sticks (or is it mullions?).

The sticks (as I'm going to call them from this moment forth) are small components that need to be carefully cut and jointed. Whenever you deal with small components like this it's a good idea to mill up some extra stock in case of damage, warping or breakage. When you decide on a pattern you like or if you make your doors the same as this design, begin by marking the mortise locations and drill small holes to remove the waste. Same mortise procedure here but this time we're working on a much smaller scale.

Where the sticks intersect each other, they receive simple half-lap joints; the ends also get a simplified tenon — no cheek.

Drill out most of the waste and follow with 1/4" mortise chisel.

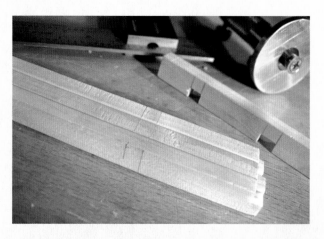

Marking out the half lap joinery for the door sticks.

ABOVE **Using a small jeweler's saw I'll cut the three sticks simultaneously.**

RIGHT **Laying things out … this can be a bit of a puzzle sometimes so take your time with it.**

Another dry fit to bring all of our new pieces together, and we'll move on to the door pulls and decorative horizontal sticks. Not that the sticks we just made aren't decorative!

I followed the same procedure used for the sticks, then shaped the handles with some moulding planes. From here you have some choices to make. Glass for the panel? Wood? Coincidentally, my sticks were lying on my workbench with a cotton cloth underneath for protection. It reminded me of the Japanese paper place on the West side of town here in Toronto. I let it sit for a day and caught up on some writing and then a day or two later, off I went. The selection was pretty overwhelming but the store was inspiring to say the least.

I decided to go with this beautiful organic-looking handmade paper that has a real fabric feel. Not in the weight but certainly in appearance. It really helped draw out the figure of the birch and walnut.

Before installing the paper panels I measure for the cabinet's back dust panel and fit it into place. Not to sound like a broken record but I originally designed and was going to do a shipped-lapped back, and will do so in the near future. I have the birch on my wood rack drying but decided for illustrational purposes (and to save some time without affecting the outer aesthetic of the piece for photographic purposes), to use an off cut of ¼" walnut plywood I've had sitting in my shop for way too long. It was originally purchased and used for a client's cabinet dust panel last year and was a suitable application for that particular piece. It will also suffice for this one now, but a solid wooden, lapped back would step up the overall appeal.

Disassemble everything, going over it all one last time with a scraper. Clean up any areas and glue. I was originally going to wedge these

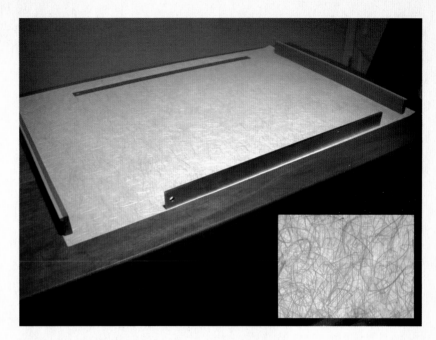

Hand made Japanese paper (Inset close-up) laid out to 'flatten'.

Checking the handle and finalizing some hinge details.

tenons but in my infinite wisdom I forgot to make the saw cuts in the tenons before I glued them.

An Experiment of Experience?
Another day or two and after a finish of oil is applied, I'll set the hinges which were off the shelf from Lee Valley. I struggled a bit with this decision and will probably change them out some time in the future (probably around the time my children are finishing up college).

I was starting to feel the calendar slip away from me and my deadline to finish off the projects and manuscript creeping in. Either that or the flu bug which was running through the city like bulls on parade and knocked the stuffing out of my family for at least half of this project. Oh Canada, eh?

The hinges work fine and are simple to install, but I'm disturbed by the barrel edges showing on the exterior of the doors while they're closed. No worries, it's my cabinet and yours is yours. My four year old already has plans for which of his Transformers will go where when it's complete.

Before I apply the paper, the final step is to drill and install some magnets for door closure. A simple quarter-inch hole is drilled and small cups that house a tiny, but powerful, magnet is pressed into the shallow recess. Rare Earth indeed! Let's move onto the panels ...

Installing the paper was pretty straightforward but I unfortunately forgot to take a photo the entire process! Sorry ... I had moved the cabinet upstairs out of my shop and my wife and I installed them in our dining room over the span of an hour or two. The friendly lady at the paper store gave me a crash course in paper application and turned me on to some Japanese paper paste. Looks like a tube of clear toothpaste with about the same consistency. I spread a layer on and rolled the paper down into the rabbets; pretty smooth except one of my sticks is warping inwards towards the back. If I were to use a glass or wood panel this wouldn't be an issue. The curve is slight and would easily push out, but the paper is well ... paper. I gently let it do its thing and after a day or two you'd never notice it as an issue.

Another few coats of finish (being careful of the paper and oil meeting) and I'll start deciding which book goes where. Cheers! We're done.

LEFT **The cabinet is working for me but the look of the hinges isn't. I'll change them when I can.**

ABOVE **Complete? Not until I change out the hinges and install the solid ship-lapped back.**

RIGHT **Top detail, the figure in this wood is incredible.**

Picture Perfect

THIS CABINET, WHILE RATHER UNASSUMING TO LOOK at, has somewhere in the neighborhood of 128 joints. If you were to count up the saw cuts to execute that many joints your arm may begin to get tired! The over-all design is not complicated, just basic mortise and tenon joinery with some bridal joints and half laps thrown in for good measure. For me the most difficult challenge when making a piece like this is keeping all of the parts straight. Properly labeled components and really accurate layout with slow, steady stock preparation should keep things going smoothly. Like always, begin with preparing the stock. Taking your time with this step, making sure your pieces are all cut to exact and accurate lengths.

Having six drawers means you have six drawer dividers, twelve runners and twelve drawer guides. I wanted to keep the front drawer dividers looking light or slim. To achieve this, and still have a fairly wide drawer supported by only ½" material, I decided to make them extra deep — 2½" deep. This in turn led to other design/construction elements. I decided to not only join them into the legs and center upright using mortise and tenons, but also to incorporate a bridal joint into the drawer guides and runners. This may sound confusing at first but we'll take it one step at a time.

Once you have all of your pieces smoothed and cross cut to length, with six sides square, begin laying out the main cabinet frame. Break up the sides-to-front and back assemblies, working your way out. I began in the top, front right-hand corner by cutting the housed dovetail into the top of the leg. I'll show the layout of this joint in the following series of photographs.

Cut list assembled, and pieces squared and to size.

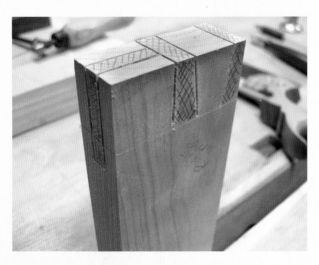

Mark out the top, front rail joinery and begin with the rip cuts.

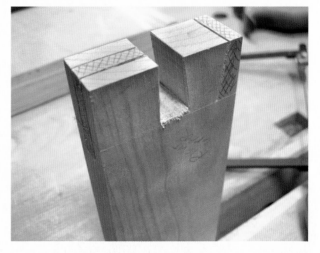

Remove the waste with a fret saw.

With the piece held in my shoulder vise I'll cross cut to establish the dovetail's outer shoulder.

Before I cut out the bridal joint portion, I'll drill some holes on the waste side to establish the top edges of the slot.

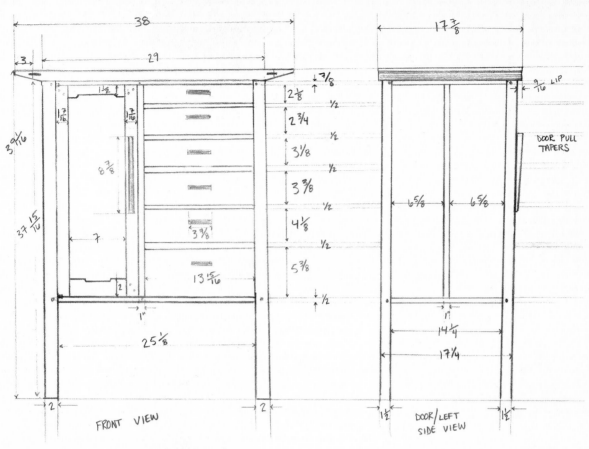

FRONT VIEW

DOOR/LEFT SIDE VIEW

DOOR PULL TAPERS

Once drilled, finish off with a few rip cuts.

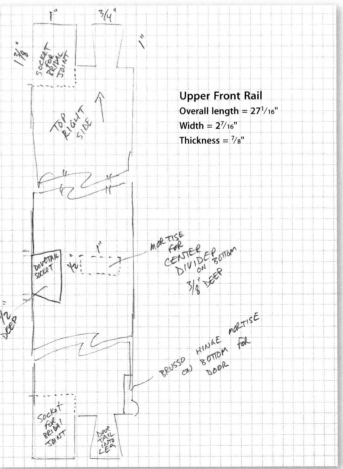

TOP RIGHT SIDE

SOCKET FOR BRIDAL JOINT

DOVETAIL SOCKET

½ DEEP

MORTISE FOR CENTER DIVIDER ON BOTTOM 3/8 DEEP

BRUSSO HINGE MORTISE ON BOTTOM FOR DOOR

SOCKET FOR BRIDAL JOINT

DOVETAIL INTO LEG

Upper Front Rail
Overall length = 27$\frac{1}{16}$"
Width = 2$\frac{7}{16}$"
Thickness = $\frac{7}{8}$"

With the rail joinery cut out, scribe the dovetails to the top of the legs. Cut and chop out the waste and then attempt a dry fit.

I know things are working well when I can take the two pieces, insert the rail's dovetail joint into the leg and hold them up unsupported horizontally as shown in this photo. This is the fit we're after! Follow the same procedure for the other legs.

LEFT **The finished rail showing dovetail and bridal joints.**

ABOVE **A nice dry fit.**

Top Frame Detail

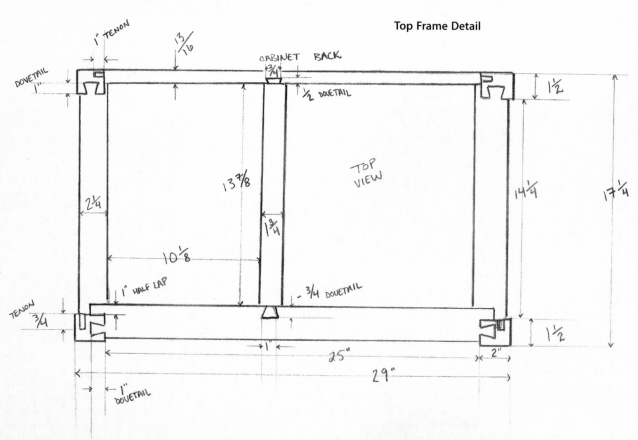

Next it's time to measure, mark and cut the side rail joinery. These get a mortise and tenon joint into the legs and the tongue portion of the bridal joint mates with the front rail.

With the top corners complete and you're happy with the way they're fitting, move on down to the main lower frame assemblies. Instead of the top dovetail joint these will get simple mortise and tenons into the leg sides. The bridal joints linking the pieces will remain constant throughout.

Cut all of the joinery for the lower rails and once again do a dry fit to check.

RIGHT **The mating side rail; follow the same procedure described above, once cut another dry fit to establish the first of four top corners.**

BELOW **Another dry fit...**

The lower rail tenon cut with bridal joint ready for completion.

Again I drill some holes to establish the outer edges of the bridal joint's open mortise.

Two of the rails ready to fit. Notice the chamfer's on the end of the tenons, to ease the fit.

With the main joinery cut and fit, I moved onto the outside panel dividers and then the front drawer dividers. These are all marked out at the same time to insure they're all at the same heights. Even a small error here would get amplified due to the sheer number of components in this piece.

The two rails fitting nicely into leg.

Another good fit; you can see how the two tenons will fit into the leg while the bridal joint wraps around the corner creating a stronger joint that will help take any wracking out of the cabinet.

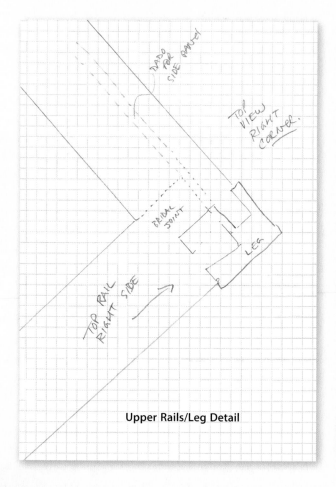

Upper Rails/Leg Detail

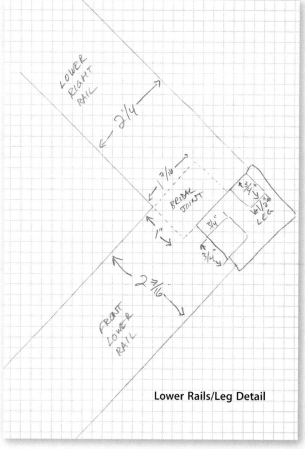

Lower Rails/Leg Detail

Once you get the hang of this split joinery idea, the cabinet begins to move along rather quickly. I think in total, all of the stock preparation and main joinery took me three days to get through. The dividers are basically the same idea as the main rails but slightly simplified. In the photo below, you can see the swiss cheese effect I'm going for with this front right leg. It not only gets the main rail mortises, but also the dozen other smaller mortises for the drawer dividers and side panel divider pieces.

The following pictures will show another example of the style of joint used for the drawer and panel dividers; a simplified version of the main frame assembly. If you count up the saw cuts you'll see this simple tenon/bridal joint has nine saw cuts alone!

The front right leg gets mortised for not only the front drawer dividers but also the side panel dividers. By the time you finish this piece your mortise chisels will feel like an extension of your hand!

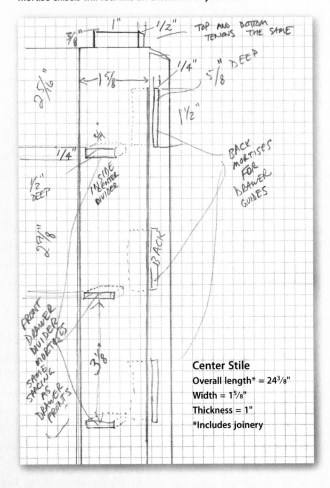

Center Stile
Overall length* = 24³⁄₈"
Width = 1⁵⁄₈"
Thickness = 1"
*Includes joinery

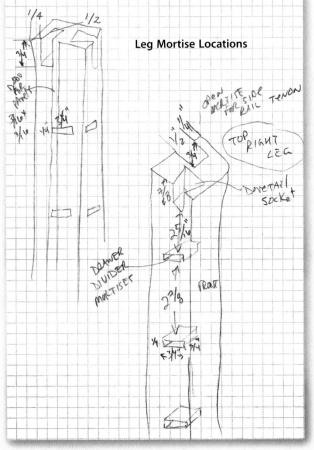

Leg Mortise Locations

Laying out one of the many dividers in this piece.

Two saw cuts will establish the cheeks.

Three more ripping cuts will determine the tenon widths.

Once again, the fret saw removes the waste.

Over to my bench hook to cross cut and remove the remaining waste of the cheeks.

Finally back to the shoulder vise to establish the tenons' shoulders. A bit of paring and this joint is ready to go. Nine cuts per side, times two ends of each divider, times twelve components. You'll be a hand-sawing master in no time at all!

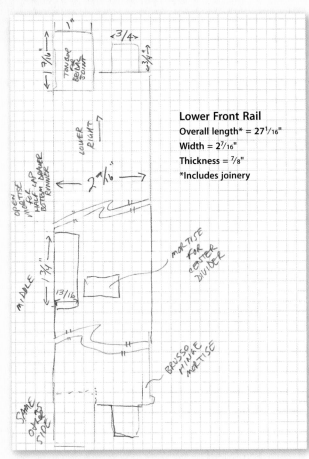

Lower Front Rail

Overall length* = 27$\frac{1}{16}$"

Width = 2$\frac{7}{16}$"

Thickness = $\frac{7}{8}$"

*Includes joinery

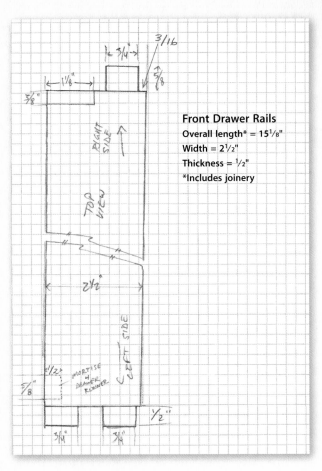

Front Drawer Rails

Overall length* = 15$\frac{1}{8}$"

Width = 2$\frac{1}{2}$"

Thickness = $\frac{1}{2}$"

*Includes joinery

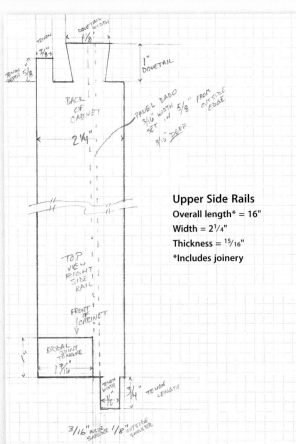

Upper Side Rails

Overall length* = 16"

Width = 2$\frac{1}{4}$"

Thickness = $\frac{15}{16}$"

*Includes joinery

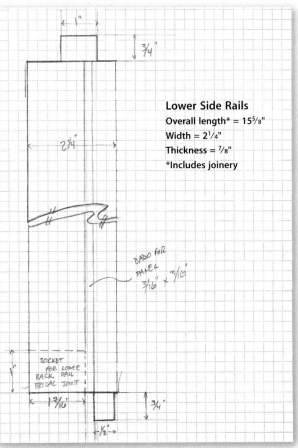

Lower Side Rails

Overall length* = 15$\frac{5}{8}$"

Width = 2$\frac{1}{4}$"

Thickness = $\frac{7}{8}$"

*Includes joinery

Work your way along following the project plans, cutting each joint and dry fitting as you go. Don't rush through any of these steps. Accurate lay out and properly-executed saw cuts will help attain a cabinet that is both square and strong.

At the top middle we'll cut a housed dovetail for a center divider. The bottom center divider/drawer runner is also slightly different than the rest of the lot. It gets a simple lap joint in the front where it meets the lower rail, and a mortise and tenon into the back lower rail. I should also mention that the back rails are turned on their edges, not kept flat like all of the other components. This is more common on furniture pieces and I'm not really sure if I had a reason for this other than some structural reinforcement.

With all of the main cabinet pieces cut and joined, we can move on to the panel joinery. Before disassembling the dry-fit cabinet, carefully label all of the pieces, top, front, this side out, that side in; whatever it takes to make sure you can get them all back together again with everything properly orientated. The panels will be captured in ¼" dados, so clearly mark their locations as well. My small plough plane will be getting a good going over from this piece.

Dry fitting the drawer and side panel dividers into the front right leg.

LEFT **Dry fitting the cabinets' frame components.**

BELOW **Ploughing out the side panel dado down into the leg. You can see I've attached a reference block for the stopped dado in the leg. Be sure you don't knock the plane into this, it serves only as a visual aid.**

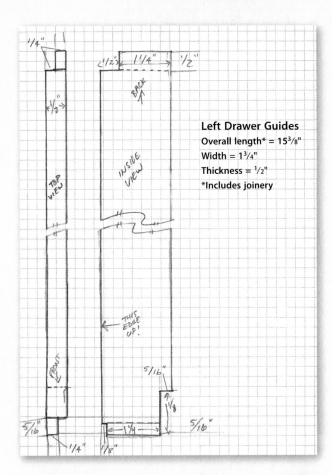

Left Drawer Guides
Overall length* = 15³/₈"
Width = 1³/₄"
Thickness = ¹/₂"
*Includes joinery

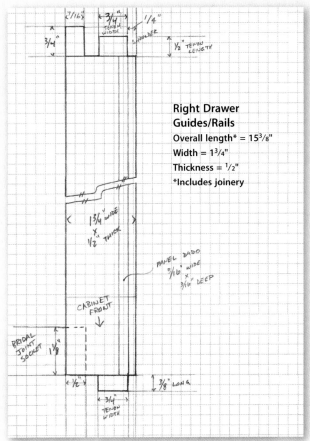

Right Drawer Guides/Rails
Overall length* = 15³/₈"
Width = 1³/₄"
Thickness = ¹/₂"
*Includes joinery

Glue and clamp up the cherry for the main cabinet top.

When the glue has set, usually over-night, surface plane and cross cut the top to finished dimension. Make sure you take into account the tongue that'll attach to the bread board ends.

With all of the dados ploughed out I'll move on to sizing and cutting out the panels, drawer fronts and main cabinet top. I'm using some ⁷/₈" cherry for the top pieces while the cabinet's side and back panels are re-claimed off cuts of ¹/₄" cherry plywood left behind from an Arts and Crafts style, kitchen cabinet build I did last year. Never throw out your off cuts! There will always be a place for them to go.

On a good day my saw will perfectly follow the scribed line as shown here. Straight, square and true. The saw pictured, an antique Disston was re-conditioned at Techno primitives. Thanks again Mark!

Cleaning the edge with a jack plane; the clamp is holding a scrap of wood at the fragile end preventing the fibers from tearing out.

With the side and back panels cut and in place, the drawer faces all sized and fit and the top dimensioned, I'll go ahead and make the door. It's a standard frame and panel with bridal joints at the corners. What else right!? My usual style of cabinet door; I'm using a glued up panel of spalted maple from the same stock as the drawer fronts. One design change on this door is I'm leaving the side stiles long as opposed to my usual method of letting the top and bottom rails run long. It seemed to fit better with the proportion of the cabinet, giving it a bit more vertical presence. Once dry fit I'll disassemble the door frame and cut a decorative shape into the upper and lower rails. A kind of 'Greene and Greene' Arts and Crafts motif that I'll carry on through some other aesthetic elements as we move on to finishing the cabinet.

The drawer's faces are made from some spalted maple from a friend back home in Cheticamp. Thanks Joel. The side and back panels are all cut and in place now as well.

LEFT The door once assembled and checked for proper fit will be disassembled and the upper and lower rails shaped.

ABOVE A little bit of Greene and Greene creeping in!

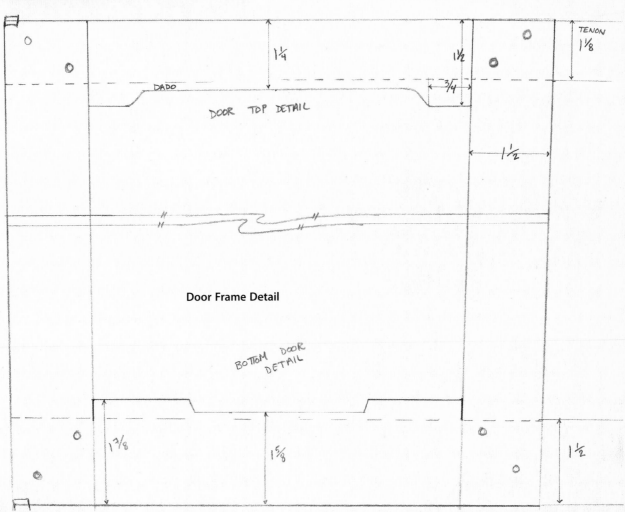

Door Frame Detail

TENON
1⅛

1¼

1½

DADO

DOOR TOP DETAIL

¾

1½

BOTTOM DOOR DETAIL

1⅞

1⅝

1½

Measure and scribe the location of the knife hinge. The pencil lines are only here for the photograph's benefit. Underneath these rough lead lines are nice, crisp scribe lines that'll make cutting out the waste much more accurate.

Lower knife hinge carefully fit into mortise.

Now that the door frame is shaped I'll go ahead and cut the mortises for the knife hinges. Once you get the hang of using knife hinges you'll never want to use anything else. These ones are manufactured by Brusso and are finely made, dead accurate and a pleasure to work with.

With the door hinges installed I'll move back to the top. We have it cut to size but now we can lay out and cut the full-width tenons, running front to back, that'll mate with the dados cut in our breadboard ends. My rabbet plane takes care of the tenon while again my small plough will handle the dado cuts.

Once the breadboards are fit and glued I'll follow the same procedure I described in Project Four, and put a bevel on the underside of the top.

Bread board detail with walnut spline installed.

Then I'll cut out two shallow pockets that will house the front walnut splines, covering the open end grain of the breadboard. Once again, a little Greene and Greene influence here perhaps?

With the top complete I'll measure and mark for some screws to hold it in place. Another nice thing about having the wide rails in the top frame is they'll serve dual purpose for attaching the top. Once drilled, make sure to elongate the holes for seasonal wood movement. Here in Ontario that could easily be up to a ¼".

For aesthetic reasons, I'll leave this next step up to you, but I removed the top from my cabinet and with spokeshaves and scrapers shape the legs to a more pleasant profile; at least to my eyes. This is done by feel, slowly taking fine shavings until the desired form is achieved. You could very easily leave the legs square, with perhaps a nice chamfer on the edges. Again design elements such as these are best left to the builder's discretion; add your own tastes and make this cabinet your own.

The same is true for the door and drawer pulls. I made mine from some walnut off-cuts but you could easily apply some store-bought hardware or come up with a design of your own. When shaping mine, I began with a long piece of stock and using a few assorted moulding planes create the profile down the entire length. Once established I'll cross cut the stock to the pulls' final width, with further shaping and refining as I go. Starting with the long stock insures continuity among the pulls.

Finish off the drawers with some dovetail joinery and install the cabinet's main compartment bottom. This will sit on top of the lower rails and receives a few wooden dowels through the back lower rail to keep it in place.

Spokeshaves; block plane and card scrapers will shape and blend the leg profile I'm after.

By working in a low light it's easy to see the shadows cast across the legs being shaped. Trusting your eye and your hand, work them to a pleasing shape, being sure to keep in mind the joinery inside; you'd hate to cut too deep!

Shaping the door pull with a small rosewood moulding plane.

Once the side profile is shaped, I'll taper the handle down its length. Once installed, this will add a unique element when viewed from the side.

With the drawers complete, the handles all made and the top and interior shelf assembled, we can go ahead and begin the glue-up process. We'll do this in stages, gluing things in sub-assemblies. Having this many pieces and joints would never be a possible glue up at one time. I started with the back assembly; the front is also glued separately and when dry I'll finish off by placing the front frame face down on the bench top and start off with the inside rails and dividers. Take your time and try to work cleanly. The less squeeze out you have, the better. With 128 joints you don't want to have to go back and re-visit each one later!

Once again the following photos will hopefully shed a little light on this labyrinth of joinery.

Upper front and side rails ready for glue.

The front leg ties in to the front and side rail joint.

A good fit … you can really notice the shaped leg profile in this shot.

Working down the leg, the uppermost drawer divider is next. This shot is looking out towards the front, from inside the cabinet.

With the front divider inserted, move on to the corresponding side-panel divider to complete the bridal joint.

Keep working your way down, assembling the joints as you go.

Opposite, center side of the top drawer divider meeting the front center upright.

You can see the center divider/drawer guide. This inside joinery differs a bit from the right side in that the drawer runner is a separate piece that'll mate with the small mortise in the back of the first divider we installed.

With the center drawer guide installed, move on to the drawer runner.

The drawer runner ready to be inserted. These are light, delicate pieces so there will be no need for a mallet today.

A good fit ... again, follow this same system down through all of the drawer components.

As mentioned I glue things up in sub-assemblies. I started off with the front and back main frames. Once dry I carefully placed the front frame assembly, face down on my bench top. Working as quickly as I could I spread glue in the joints and inserted all of the dividers, runners and guides. Then while the glue is still wet, I attached the back frame to the half completed assembly; I shouldn't have to say this but remember to insert all of the panels before the main back frame goes on ... I almost forgot and would have been left with an open post and panel cabinet. This was actually an appealing thought for a while but then I remembered I'd have all of those empty dados everywhere. Maybe glass panels would be nice in this piece. Unfortunately, it wasn't in the budget so my off cut pieces of plywood will have to make do for this prototype.

Sub-assembly glue up. Front main frame.

Before the glue is completely cured I'll go around and check for any squeeze out. Keeping your work clean as you go will make the finishing process a bit more enjoyable.

Once the glue has set I'll drill and install a dozen or so walnut dowels, these will insure the joints will stay put for many, many years to come.

RIGHT Getting ready for the final assembly. On top of the bench is the front frame, safely lying face down on some old towels. Next to it, all laid out in order from top to bottom are the cabinet cross pieces. There in the foreground, just in front of my bench is the back of the cabinet frame assembly. These two main frame components are all glued up and just need to be linked. Notice I didn't put a back panel behind the drawers? In my world this cabinet will come to be an entertainment unit and will probably house a bit of electronic equipment. I wanted a panel for the main door side but decided to leave it out from behind the drawers. This will allow for some ventilation later on.

BELOW Final assembly and glue up.

Side view of drawers and door pulls. These half blinds are quite subtle with the tones of the spalted maple drawer fronts and that of the interior butternut being similar. In the future I'd use more contrasting wood species. Really, if you're going to go through all of the time to cut out those dovetails; they might as well jump out at you when you open the drawer's right? Perhaps this subdued approach works better for this piece giving it a gentler more sophisticated feel … I'll leave it up to you to decide. Enjoy the process!

Post and panel detail with
drawers in place.

Where the Hunters Heal

THIS HUNT BOARD, OR SIDEBOARD AS MOST people tend to call it, follows some traditional design rules with it's overall dimension and height, but I've attempted to transform the classic look and feel of the piece into something more modern with straight, simple lines and exposed joinery. The contrasting cherry and walnut work well together adding to the whole 'handmade modern' aesthetic. Speaking of wood, let's begin there, at the stock preparation. Assemble your cut list and get things squared and smooth ...

I started with the main carcass construction by laying out and cutting the dovetails. Keep in mind the stub tenons at the front and back corners that will be mortised into the legs once the dovetailing is completed. For no reason other than visual, I decided to cut small dovetails at the top edges and larger tails on the bottom. I actually used the top panel as a template for the bottom once I finished cutting out the tails and simply skipped every other one. That way the spacing would be exactly the same from a side view perspective.

LEFT **Flattening the top cabinet panel with my Jack plane.**

ABOVE **Cross cut to finished length.**

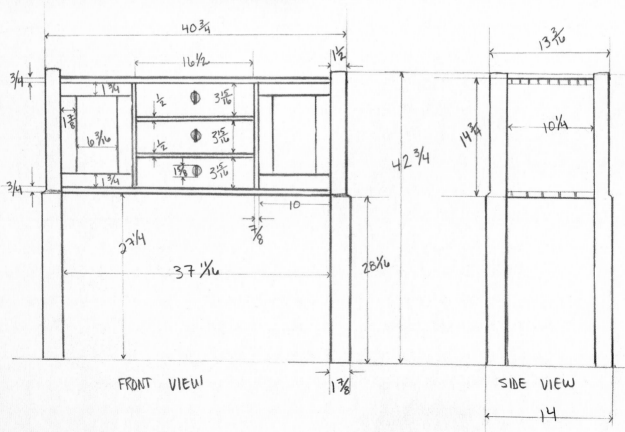

Planing the freshly trimmed edge, note the maple block clamped to the end — this will help eliminate any tear out.

Once the tails are all cut and cleaned out I'll plough out the grooves for the two sliding doors. They'll run in the same dado always remaining on the same plane. When complete I move to the back of the panels to cut a rabbet that will register and create a recess for the cabinets back panel later on. Once the plough plane work is complete I'll prep the door frame pieces and assemble the interior dividers.

A sea of orange holds the interior dividers together while the glue sets up. I used some poplar as a secondary wood for these components with a 3" cherry strip on the front show side.

With the dovetails complete we'll cut out the rabbets and dados.

I ended up using some poplar jointed onto some narrower cherry stock which will be seen on the cabinet front. This being the final project for the book and watching my lumber pile dwindle away here at my shop; I thought it would be a good idea to use a secondary wood on the interior, unseen portion of the case.

Mark out and cut the mortises in the top and bottom panels that will house the two dividers. I used a large router plane and finished with my mortise chisel, to execute this stepped groove. Once complete I transferred the mortise over to the dividers and cut out the rabbets followed by some backsaw work to establish the tenons.

A dry fit with the basic carcass complete, and we can now go back and work on the center drawer divider assembly.

Cut and fit the dividers; then mark out and cut the mortise and tenons. Follow with the drawer runners which get a shallow tenon set into the back of the drawer dividers and then will receive some dowels down the inside of the main dividers. This will be plenty strong enough for this application.

Begin the interior divider dados with a few light passes with a router plane. Once the sides are well established I'll cut down to depth and chop out the remaining mortises that will house the tenons.

The interior divider joinery. This pattern is repeated at both the top and bottoms of the dividers.

ABOVE **One of two drawer dividers being cut.**

RIGHT **One of the four mortises for the drawer dividers.**

I decided to add a pocket hole in the back top of the main carcass dividers. I use a Kregg pocket hole jig with a special 'stepped' bit held in my brace. These modern day jigs are usually associated with the power tool shop but I find they work great in my hand tool-only work space.

Another dry fit, with the interior drawer components complete we can disassemble and begin laying out the joinery for the carcass sides to legs. This again, like the main interior dividers, gets a stepped mortise and tenon. Carefully scribe and chop out the full length of the grooves. Then go back and chop down into the groove bottom, establishing the mortises within. Once chopped and cleaned, transfer the mortise locations over to the cabinet side panels. Rabbet the edges and cut the tenons to fit.

Another dry fit and we'll shape the shoulders in the legs. This step is accomplished by first laying out deep scribe lines to establish the upper width of each leg.

A pocket hole jig, usually found in the power tool shop works quite well with my old brace driving this dedicated bit.

Drawer runners get tenoned into the back of the dividers and doweled into the main divider sides.

Cutting the tenons into the rabbeted carcass side; this will join into the leg.

Deep scribe lines will establish the shoulders on the upper portion of the legs.

Then follow with a series of saw cuts across and down to meet the line. Turn the leg over and with your widest bench chisel carefully chop out the waste. Clean as much as you can with a hand plane but the lower few inches, just above the shoulder, will need to be dressed with scrapers and spokeshave.

Clean up the shoulders where the leg steps to its bottom portion.

Saw cuts will establish the depth and make chopping out the waste a whole lot easier.

Carcass-to-leg joinery cut out.

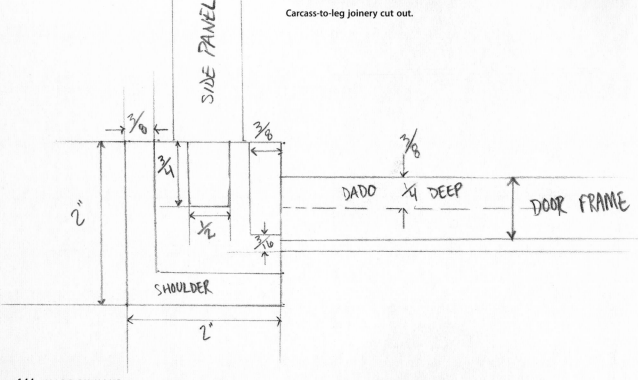

Leg joinery detail.

Top right corner, stub tenon detail plus carcass dry fit.

Dry fit of main carcass and legs.

Now we can move on to finishing the doors and building the drawers. The doors in the cabinet are an extremely simple, butt joined and dowel assembly. I'm sure woodworking purists will cringe when they see this, but the reality is this type of joinery, for this particular application, is more than acceptable. The doors will never "open"; they don't have to hang or swing and should never have any real wracking type of force on them. All they'll really do in life is slide gracefully from side to side, captured in the dado. So with that in mind, cut the pieces to proper lengths and then the cut the rabbets to create the sliding runners on the top and bottom rails. Take shallow passes and check the rabbet widths as you go. A nice fit here is important; too tight and you'll curse it every time you slide a door open; too loose and you'll feel and hear that sloppy fit every time it's open. Again, take your time here when fitting this joint to insure a nice sliding action on the doors.

Once we achieve that perfect fit we're after, cut a bead into the edge of the top and bottom rails. Any time I build a piece with sliding doors I'll try to put a bead where they meet the main carcass body; this will help hide any slight imperfections while the doors travel across the cabinet's width.

Plough out the dado on the inside door frames that will hold the panels. Next I'll take the four door stiles and plane them down so they're slightly thinner in thickness than the door rails; this simple detail creates a pleasing shadow line that will accentuate the beads and overall look of the piece. From here, drill for the dowels and assemble. With the doors complete, move on to the drawers. But first I'll cut the legs to final length, and finish off any smoothing at the shoulders.

Cutting the rabbets into the door rails.

A bead is cut into the door rails.

Hardwood dowels are plenty strong to hold the door pieces together.

Another dry fit to check that the doors are sliding freely.

Three solid wooden drawers all dovetailed with half blind in the front and through dovetails in the back. No surprises here, besides, you should be a master at making traditional style dovetailed drawers by now right?

For the drawer pulls I bored out a $1^3/8$" hole into the center of each drawer. Then with some small cherry off cuts I made a small 'pull' that gets a kind of tenon cut into the back. This small tenon will fit snugly into the drilled hole and give you somewhere to grasp when opening the drawers. A single cut nail down through the drawer top and into the pull top, in conjunction with the snug fit is all that's needed to safely hold together.

While I'm on the topic of drawer pulls I should mention that my original design had some similar door

I'll edge plane all of the drawer side together.

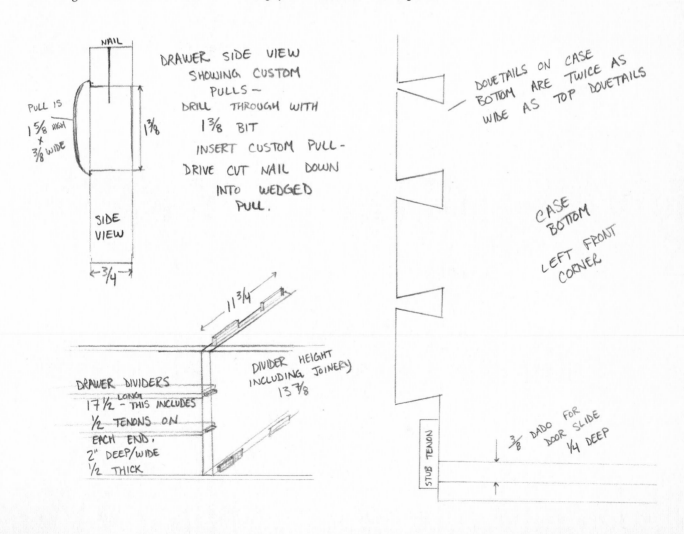

NAIL

PULL IS
$1^5/8$ HIGH
x
$3/8$ WIDE

$1^3/8$

SIDE VIEW

←— $3/4$ —→

DRAWER SIDE VIEW
SHOWING CUSTOM
PULLS —
DRILL THROUGH WITH
$1^3/8$ BIT
INSERT CUSTOM PULL —
DRIVE CUT NAIL DOWN
INTO WEDGED
PULL.

$11^3/4$

DRAWER DIVIDERS
$17^1/2$ LONG — THIS INCLUDES
$1/2$ TENONS ON
EACH END.
2" DEEP/WIDE
$1/2$ THICK

DIVIDER HEIGHT
INCLUDING JOINERY
$13^7/8$

DOVETAILS ON CASE
BOTTOM ARE TWICE AS
WIDE AS TOP DOVETAILS

CASE
BOTTOM
LEFT FRONT
CORNER

STUB TENON

$3/8$ DADO FOR
DOOR SLIDE
$1/4$ DEEP

pulls; but once I reached this stage of the game I felt they really didn't need it. The slight step between the doors frame and panel is enough to gently slide the doors open. One last dry fit and we should be ready to start the final glue up.

Do this in stages, with the main carcass body being first. Remember to get the doors in place before attaching the top! If you forget this step now they'll never fit into the opening between the cabinets' top and bottom. Take your time and once dry attach the legs. Let stand overnight and in the morning we'll address the back panel.

The cabinet back is simply cut from some more cherry plywood off cuts and inserted between the rabbets we cut earlier. A few small nails will hold it in place.

From here it's a few coats of oil/varnish and we're done.

Cheers!

RIGHT **Chopping out the waste of a half blind dovetail in the drawer front.**

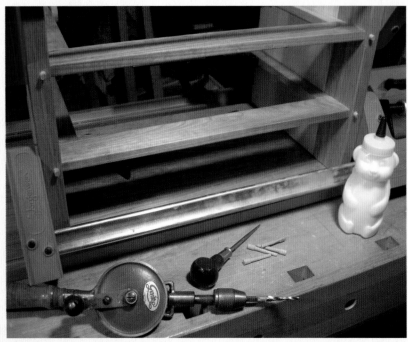

Glue and clamp ... I'll drill and drive some dowels through the tenons while they're still clamped up.

Once the glue has set, I'll cut the dowels using a Japanese style flush cut saw.

ABOVE **A good look at the drawer pulls, and the great contrast between the walnut drawer fronts and the drawer sides.**

LEFT **I like the smooth shoulder on the leg and the bead on the door rails is another nice detail.**

Afterthoughts — June 17, 2009

IT WAS MONDAY APRIL 7TH, 2008. THAT was the day I was first contacted by Megan Fitzpatrick asking if I'd be interested in working on a project with Popular Woodworking Books. She suggested I contact the editor, David Thiel and that both she and Chris (Schwarz) recommended me for the job. Thankfully, my inflated ego lifted me back up off of the floor when my jaw dropped down to greet it!

I was still in Cape Breton, with my wife and two children. We were feeling somewhat drained after coming through four long winters of having kids, splitting fire wood, building wooden boats, stacking firewood, eating, drinking and being merry for the most part while we weren't thinking about moving the firewood from here to there ... living on love you might say — the fire wood, our only source of heat to keep warm through those harsh North Atlantic winters.

It was around this same time my wife, Carolyn and I had decided it beneficial for our two young children to be able to experience this wonderful rural living on Cape Breton Island as well as the cultures, the colors and the opportunities of a city. We made up our minds to relocate to downtown Toronto for the ten month school year and enjoy summers back on Cape Breton in our home, a hundred-year-old wooden house on forty acres in paradise which I'm sure we'll renovate until we're buried there ... but that hopefully won't be for another million seasons or so, we still have so much more to write about and the firewood is getting low you know?

You've got to love the seasons with the trees and the tides ever changing; that's where I find my inspiration. This is what I live for, teaching our children the ways of the world and all of its differences and beauty. Working with their hands and their hearts, finding pride in creation and respect for the planet and the working hand. An honest day where they can still get dirty while imagining the impossible and day dreaming of knowledge through education; my wife is a school teacher and well, you know what I do to get by, so this is how we've afforded this luxury of living.

So back to the story of starting the journey from boat shop to subway but working wood throughout; this was around the time I decided I wasn't bringing the power tools with me. No shop space to speak of in the city and I really didn't know what circumstances may arise. I'd build with my hands like my grandfathers did before me, what better way than while writing a book on the topic. The topic I was given, building furniture using hand tools, and from there the freedom to fly. David, my editor stepped back and said nothing but gave confidence and guidance right from the start.

It's been over a year since that initial contact and here I am in the final stages of editing and tonight, on a rainy day in June, I'm writing some more...

Proof reading and living with these projects and pages for three months now (the book was finished on the 6th of March) I'm finally on with new projects and developments, still in the basement and still only using hand tools. I'm wondering if you the reader, when you get to these pages would you have yet made any of these pieces. Spent time with the tools in your own work shops at home, planing the grain through shavings and illustration. Figuring cut lists and board foot I'm smiling now, wishing you the best and encouraging you to share the experience.

Even if you didn't swing a hammer or sharpen an iron but plugged in the table saw and router; what ever is working for you in your own shop is fine with me at either end. Seriously, this picture I create through words on a page, the romanticism of working wood by hand is because I like what I do and I do what I like. It's how I am currently working through my own personal development as a woodworker and furniture designer. I'm not trying to wave any flags and get you to run out and pawn off the power tools. It's kind of like eating Christmas dinner at a relative's place when they know I'm vegetarian and don't eat any meat. Some people get all nervous that they're making me sick, chewing the fat across the table from me. Not at all really, I couldn't care less. To each his own and the woodshop is the same; because I am using only hand tools on these projects is my own circumstances and choices. Make up your own mind and enjoy the process of creating with wood for yourself and your family. Follow your own path but please let me know, I'd love to see some examples of the projects ... especially if you used power tools to do it with!

I'm really enjoying the furniture that sits here in my house, made in the basement just out of sight. Our family and friends have given encouraging feedback but I'm my own worst critic when it comes to these things. I'll change a few elements in the sideboard I think ... I still consider these six projects my prototypes, still evolving and changing from one model to the next, this is the intoxication created from woodcraft and design, iron and steel pushing the grain. Maybe you've already made some changes of your own, the design evolving while you worked your way through your own interpretations on these forms.

The tool chest I'll make a little bit larger the next time around to accommodate some more

of those damn 'essential' hand tools. I thought I had all that I needed and then so and so, or such and such went and made another one ... another 'essential' waiting to work ... I warned you they'd be addictive!

The small side table, those skinny legs and all, is my favorite now looking back. I've already designed three variations on this form adding some inlay and alternative leg shapes. Larger drawer boxes and a taller entry table version; real-skinny legs and all I should call it. You'll have to wait for the next book for that one! It's really an endless cycle and when you stumble across a piece that is working, both aesthetically and practically, it becomes a real pleasure to build. This piece in particular is a lot of fun to make.

The post and panel cabinet with all of its joinery still brings a smile when I walk past it. Lots of hours spent in figuring and labeling all of those components, it proudly stands in our dining room, full of our children's favorite things. One of the drawers swelled up a bit these past few months and 'someone' pulled the drawer handle off trying to open it; no worries, I'll just fix it ... that's what I do, this is what I love.

The wall cabinet is pleasant and I'll never build two the same. This isn't because of any complaints in this design but for me, the nature of a small cabinet should never be duplicated; small objects of art, with one-off uniqueness.

The book cabinet with doors does just what I asked, holds my favorite titles away from the dust and tiny hands, potential tearing and spilling, or God forbid, cracking spines and worse: dog-ears! I still have to change out those hinges; it's on my list ... seriously. Those doors moved a little bit as well and I think I'll have to take a few light shavings off of the inside edges. It'll be nice when I find the time to carry it back down the stairs, into the workshop for a final-fine tuning and then calling it done. I'll need to build another one soon enough though, to a larger dimension again for more books. Every time I get a commission or find a few extra dollars I try to pick up a new book or DVD.

Working wood is truly a lifetime spent learning, one labor of love with the wood full of secrets. I just thought of the years to come and the work I still want to do, a life time ahead, will I have time? Sam Maloof passed away last month at the age of 93, a living testament to the love of the work; a Woodworker or one who is working with wood, I can only hope to be as fortunate as he to live all those years, working with my hands, truly doing what I love and then perhaps in my case, writing it down and sharing the experience, the stories and the knowledge.

This I believe is why we chose this path, to feel the hand swinging the hammer; then blow by blow we'll follow the road on down through this working wood.

Happy shavings and thank you for reading.

For current information on my work you can find me on the internet at:
www.theunpluggedwoodshop.com

GALLERY

The following gallery represents some of my first steps into furniture making. These photographs were taken by Don Carstens, my good friend and next-door-neighbour on Cape Breton Island. Thanks again neighbour.

Recipe Box on Stand

My wife wanted me to make her a recipe box for Christmas one year, this was what I came up with. This piece is probably the very first time I sat down with pencil and paper and actually 'designed' a piece of furniture. From vision, to sketch, to cut list this was my beginning. It was built using power tools and was a learning curve for me to use local hard wood, including drying and stacking to resawing and dimensioning. A little rough around the edges, but my heart was in the right place. It still sits in our kitchen being used for its intended purpose. The wood used is bird's eye maple for the carcass and white oak for the stand; both from Frasers Mill here in Cape Breton (thanks David!) He always let me rummage through 'that old pile in the back' to search for hidden treasures of maple, oak and sometimes ash. The drawer fronts and doors are walnut.

Tool Chest (The Widow Maker)

When it came time for me to relocate my shop from Cape Breton to Toronto I needed a way to carry along my hand tool essentials. I didn't yet know the size of my new work space so a portable tool chest was required. This one holds most of the tools I need and now in conjunction wth my Cabinetmakers Toolchest, my wood shop is mobile and efficient. This design was manufactured with power tools over a day or two. When full it weighs a ton but it's better than getting to a work site and not having a specific tool on hand!

The chest is Cherry with Birch interior components. The outside panels were brushed with vinegar and steel wool — a 'green' solution for ebonising wood. Contact me if you want the recipe!

Shabby Chic — Shaker Style

These next two pieces are my initial steps with using hand tools to build furniture. Both are Shaker pieces and were projects I found in books and articles. Shaker style can lend itself so well to almost any setting and really compliment the hand-tool-only woodshop.

The large five-drawer table is an interpretation of a Garrett Hack design. I think this was his interpretation of a Shaker interpretation of a Japanese interpretation of ... you get the idea; timeless. A nice design to learn the basics of small table joinery. Lots of dovetails and storage for such a compact piece. The drawer fronts are some local maple and the carcass is cherry.

The small single drawer Saturday Table is my version of a design from Kerry Pierce's beautiful book, *Pleasant Hill Shaker Furniture*. This piece was a lot of fun to make and probably influenced my initial inspiration for Skinny Legs and All ... The wood is cherry with the drawer front and aprons of walnut.

Both of these pieces are in our main living space here on the coast and still get all of the daily abuse of living life with solid wooden furniture. They'll grow old gracefully with lots of life around them. Both Garrett Hack and Kerry Pierce are incredible craftsmen and authors and I'd recommend reading anything they have to offer.

THE COMPLETE WOODWORKER

THE PRACTICAL WOODWORKER

MODERN PRACTICAL JOINERY — George Ellis — Linden Publishing

The Art of Joinery — Moxon

Aldren A. Watson — HAND TOOLS

Making & Mastering WOOD PLANES — Finck

Workbenches FROM DESIGN & THEORY TO CONSTRUCTION & USE

James Krenov — THE IMPRACTICAL CABINETMAK

ROY UNDERHILL THE WOODWRIGHT'S APPRENTICE
Twenty Favorite Projects from The Woodwright's Shop

A Cabinetmaker's Notebook

David Charlesworth's FURNITURE-MAKING TECHNIQUES VOLUME TWO
David Charlesworth's FURNITURE-MAKING TECHNIQUES
David Charlesworth's Furniture-making Techniques
David Charlesworth's Furniture-making Techniques

Fine Art of Cabinetmak

REFERENCES

This is a list of tool suppliers where I've purchased the tools used throughout these projects. Also, at left is a photo of some of the books that I've found useful in my woodworking journey.

Lie-Nielsen Toolworks
For, in my opinion, the finest quality hand tools on the market today, you can't go wrong with these ones. Hand planes, chisels and back saws, you won't be disappointed.
www.lie-nielsen.com

Lee Valley Tools
A great Canadian company with everything you'll need to get started! Great mail order service as well as the Veritas line of fine tools.
www.leevalley.com

Tools for Working Wood
This is where I purchased my bow saw by Gramercy tools; a great website and blog as well.
www.toolsforworkingwood.com

Japan Woodworker
Another on-line woodworking resource it's where I purchased my moulding planes. They have an entire catalogue of hand tools.
www.japanwoodworker.com

FOR RECONDITIONED HAND SAWS AND DRILLS:
www.technoprimitives.com
Mark Harrell does an amazing job restoring and sharpening hand saws. You may find he has some for sale as well. Check out his website (now the home of Bad Axe Tool Works) for more details and tell him I sent you!

www.wktools.com
This is where I got my incredible Millers Falls egg beater style drill. It's over 100 years old but looks brand new!

MORE GREAT TITLES FROM POPULAR WOODWORKING!

 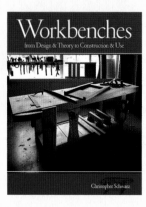 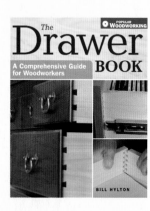 

HANDPLANE ESSENTIALS	**WORKBENCHES**	**THE DRAWER BOOK**	**GROVE PARK INN ARTS & CRAFTS FURNITURE**
By Christopher Schwarz	*By Christopher Schwarz*	*By Bill Hylton*	*By Bruce Johnson*

HANDPLANE ESSENTIALS

By Christopher Schwarz

Handplane Essentials contains everything you need to choose the right tool for your budget and project, take it out of the box, sharpen it and use it successfully. Compiled from more than 10 years of the author's writing on the subject of handplanes, learn the basics, sharpening, techniques, the history and philosophy and handplanes, and read product reviews.

ISBN 13: 978-1-44030-298-5
ISBN 10: 1-44030-298-7
hardcover, 312 p., #Z6650

WORKBENCHES

By Christopher Schwarz

Workbenches shows you how to design and build a good workbench and most importantly, how to use it in your shop for all sorts of tasks. This book dives deep into the historical records of the 18th and 19th centuries and teaches about traditional designs that are simpler than modern benches, easier to build and perfect for both power and hand tools.

ISBN 13: 978-1-55870-840-2
ISBN 10: 1-55870-840-5
hardcover, 144 p., # Z1981

THE DRAWER BOOK

By Bill Hylton

No detail exemplifies the quality of a piece of furniture better than a drawer; and no other aspect of furniture making causes as much anxiety. *The Drawer Book* gives you foolproof steps to create every kind of drawer, with every kind of woodworking joint, as well as professional information on the best way to fit and mount every drawer.

ISBN 13: 978-1-55870-842-6
ISBN 10: 1-55870-842-1
hardcover, 160 p., #Z2007

GROVE PARK INN ARTS & CRAFTS FURNITURE

By Bruce Johnson

The Grove Park Inn opened in 1913 and was decorated with Arts & Crafts furniture from Roycroft. The Inn retains many of the original pieces and has acquired a large and rare collection of original Arts & Crafts furniture. Includes never-before-published measured drawings. A wonderful collection for history buffs.

ISBN 13: 978-1-55870-849-5
ISBN 10: 1-55870-849-9
hardcover, 176 p., # Z2279

These and other great woodworking books are available at your local bookstore, woodworking stores or from online suppliers.

www.popularwoodworking.com